LA MADRE
The life and spirituality of Teresa of Avila

Reflect, for it is true,
that God gives himself to those
who give up everything for him.

St Teresa

Elizabeth Ruth Obbard

LA MADRE

The life and spirituality of Teresa of Avila

ST PAULS

Unless otherwise indicated extracts from the writings of St Teresa in this book are taken from the translation of the *Complete Works* by Professor E. Allison Peers, published by Sheed and Ward and used with permission.

ST PAULS
Middlegreen, Slough SL3 6BT, United Kingdom
Moyglare Road, Maynooth, Co. Kildare, Ireland

© ST PAULS (UK) 1994

ISBN 085439 468 0

Printed by Biddles Ltd, Guildford

ST PAULS is an activity of the priests and brothers of the Society of St Paul who proclaim the Gospel through the media of social communication

Contents

Introduction

There are many ways to write the life of a saint, mine perforce has been selective. Too often I feel that accounts of Teresa the woman are sidetracked into long accounts of each individual convent she founded. Teresa certainly led an incredibily rich and varied life, but in trying to describe everything, she herself is submerged in the welter of events.

I have therefore simplified or stressed various aspects of her life, in this way hoping to present a truer portrait than is sometimes given when overmuch attention is paid to detail.

I am neither Spanish scholar nor professional historian, simply a woman who has lived at first hand the way of Carmel inaugurated by *La Madre*. Thus I can testify to her balanced humanity and wisdom because they have impinged on me pratically over the past years.

Teresa was no narrow-minded fanatic. Her breadth of vision, warmth of emotion, passion for God, are as inspiring today as they have ever been. She is a woman of flesh and blood, true, vital and endearing. And her legacy remains in the living spirit of her Carmelite daughters and sons – to these, who are my sisters and brothers in a special way, I dedicate this book.

The foundation of St Teresa of Avila

Prologue

It was dark and bitterly cold in the early hours of a Spanish spring morning as Don Alonso de Cepeda paced the ground floor of his family mansion in the old Jewish quarter of the city of Avila. Upstairs, attended by a midwife and her personal maid, his twenty year old wife, Doña Beatriz de Ahumada, lay in labour with her third child. The candlelight flickered on the thick walls, throwing Don Alonso's shadow back and forth on the fine tapestries and heavy oak furnishings.

At length the door opened and the midwife looked in. Dropping a deep curtsey she murmured respectfully "All is well sir, my lady has been safely delivered, God and his mother be praised". Don Alonso nodded gravely. Slowly he climbed the stairs as the maid appeared with a jug of hot water and preceded him into the chamber. He turned his gaze to his young wife almost hidden in the damask drapery of the high matrimonial bed with the baby nestling against her breast. A thatch of jet black hair peeped out from the swaddling bands. "It's a girl" whispered the mother as Don Alonso glimpsed for the first time the infant who was to become his best loved child.

He walked to the window and gazed over the city, noticing that the first rays of dawn were beginning to lighten the sky, throwing the encircling city walls and the boulders of the plain into sharp relief.

He was not a man of many words. He had done his duty in providing his wife with every care for her confinement; now he was embarrassed to linger in this female atmosphere with its odour of birth and blood. He bowed to Doña Beatriz and the baby with due solemnity, then went downstairs and took the large family record book off the shelf. There were not many entries in it as yet, for Don Alonso's past was such as was better hidden, buried in the mercy of God. He knew well that his compatriots were not merciful towards those with such a background as he had inherited. His fine Jewish profile was a constant reminder of it and he hoped vaguely that this little daughter of his would grow up with her mother's fragile beauty and pure Spanish features, safe from the prying questions of inquisitive or unsympathetic neighbours. He smoothed the page absentmindedly then wrote with deliberation the following words: "On Wednesday the twenty-eighth of March 1515, at five o'clock in the morning within half an hour or so of daybreak, my daughter Teresa was born". Then he poured and drank a glass of wine, little guessing that he had fathered a child who would make his own name renowned – a new Avilese woman destined to become a saint.

Six days later the infant was baptised in the parish church of St John, the very day that the first Mass was celebrated at the Convent of the Incarnation, built outside the city walls on the site of the erstwhile Jewish cemetery and synagogue.

The rest of Teresa's life was in some way an exploration of what that baptismal ceremony meant, the death and resurrection process involved in becoming fully one with the Lord who had chosen her to follow him, the One who came "not to call the just but sinners". Of this Teresa was intensely conscious, for after her death her breviary was found to contain this inscription: "On Wednesday, feast of Saint Berthold of the Order of Carmelites, on the twenty-ninth (sic) day of March 1515 at five in the morning was born Teresa of Jesus, the sinner."

The Spain of La Santa

The Spain in which Teresa de Cepeda y Ahumada found herself was the proud inheritor of a long and unique tradition. Cut off by the Pyrenees from the rest of Europe, open in the south to invasion from North Africa, Spain had developed over the centuries not only a strongly nationalistic Catholicism but also a rich culture with Moorish and Jewish elements.

From the seventh to the eleventh centuries the Moors had been in the ascendancy, especially in the south around Cordoba. They had introduced Arabic as the official language with Mozarabic, a Romance dialect with many Semitic loan words, as the common *lingua franca* of Arab, Christian and Jew alike. The eleventh century saw a concentrated Christian counteroffensive which regained many important towns for Castile (Avila and Toledo among them) and resulted in a promotion of the Latin and Spanish tongues, but Moorish influence remained strong. It was Spanish clerics who first translated the works of Aristotle and his Arabic commentators Avicenna (980-1037) and Averoës (1126-1198) into Latin and thus paved the way for the theology of the great Thomas Aquinas.

With Moslem influence was coupled that of the Jews, always better treated in the Arab world. When Northern Europe was involved in the Crusades, intent on rescuing the Holy Places from the Turks, the Spaniards had more than enough to contend with in their own country and were uninterested in further holy wars. Their situation enabled them to avoid much of the anti-Semitic feeling aroused by popular preachers in the rest of Europe. Jews fled to Spain to escape the pogroms and persecutions initiated elsewhere by the crusaders. Their numbers were again increased by those fleeing the hysteria attendant upon the Black Death, which fanatics attributed to Jews poisoning the wells. Alas, the haven they found in Spain was not to last. 1391 saw the massacre of thousands of Jews in Seville, and from that time onwards their lot was one of increasing misery until their final expulsion in 1492. Spain, newly awakened to a sense of nationhood, equated Catholicism with patriotism; there was no place for the "outsider".

As for the Moors, they were gradually pushed back towards Africa. The defence of Granada, twenty three years before Teresa's birth, was their last great battle and it left the Spaniards victorious. Ferdinand of Aragon, husband of Isabelle of Castile and now joint ruler of a united Spain, rejoiced over this crowning triumph. In his youth he had boasted "I will pluck out all the seeds from that Granada" (Granada = pomegranate) and he lived to see his boast fulfilled. Subjugated and humiliated, Moors were employed in menial tasks or waited as slaves on Christian masters. After their defeat at Granada revolts were sporadic and ineffective; the Moors were no longer a people to reckon with.

Meanwhile the pope had granted the Spanish sovereigns the right to set up and direct the Inquisition, a system of courts to control churchmen and ensure orthodox teaching. It was under the direct authority of the King and there could be no appeal to Rome against the verdict. Almost immediately a purge of convert Moors and Jews was set in motion as these formed a powerful middle class of traders and financiers. Spain did not persue her policies on the religious front alone; her efforts would culminate in the infamous statutes regarding purity of blood which reached proportions far exceeding what was originally envisaged when the Inquisition was launched. What seems ludicrous to us, is that this was all carried out by men to personally often lived lives of great moral rectitude and piety (or perhaps, if we were familiar with the Gospels we would be less surprised and have a sense of *déja vue* after all).

In such a climate, to be a Moor or a Jew was to find oneself an object of hatred and suspicion, and to be a convert to Christianity because one was in terror of losing one's life and livelihood, was not much better. Being a Jewish convert – a *marrano* (literally 'pig'), one of contaminated mixed descent, created an enormous social gap. Integration into Christian society was difficult and the *marrano* was a constant prey to suspicious neighbours or rivals who could possibly denounce a whole family to the authorities as unorthodox.

In 1485 the Inquisitors were in Toledo to search out "new Christians" suspected of being Judaisers or clinging to Jewish practises in secret. Those who came forward to "confess" would be spared after suitable public penance, those who did not and were reported by others would feel the full weight of the secular arm at the subsequent *autos da fé*.

Among those who 'confessed' and partook in the public humiliation before being officially reconciled to the Church was a certain Juan Sanchez, silk merchant, and his sons. Barefooted, wearing the degrading yellow *sanbenitas*, they were paraded through the streets of Toledo before acknowledging their 'crimes' in the imposing Cathedral, watched by an assembled crowd avid to view the discomfiture of respectable citizens. It was this Juan Sanchez who was to be the grandfather of Teresa, and one of his sons, Alonso, her beloved father.

A number of years after this demeaning spectacle the Sanchez family moved away from the city of their public disgrace to try and make a new life for themselves in Avila. Avila, perched like an enormous rocky castle on the hill beside the river Adaja and commanding a view over the vast plains surrounding it, was itself a microcosm of Castilian history. Recaptured from the Moors at the same time as Toledo – 1085 – it was resettled by knights from Burgos, Leon, Asturias and Galicia. Well did it merit its title "Avila of the Knights". The enclosing wall, begun almost immediately, was the work in part of Moorish captives, and its fine cathedral apse was an intrinsic part of the city fortifications, melding in its stones religious and national aspirations. Within the walls trade flourished and there were many stories of the valour of the knights who continued to defend the city fiercely against Arab attack. In the thirteenth century legend tells how Avila was saved from the enemy encamped without by a certain woman, Jimena Blasquez, who, with the men away, summoned the women to the battlements and herself rode all night round the walls calling "My kinswomen, do like me and God will give us the victory!" "God had placed in her heart" says an ancient account of the episode "great daring, for she seemed rather a valiant chieftain than a woman". Teresa was to take up the cry when she urged her nuns to be "as strong men" and not lack courage in their personal battle with the forces of evil:

> In our conflict we cannot be forced to surrender by hunger. We may die but we cannot be conquored.[1]

Avila was an important city of Castile in Teresa's time, with crowded, narrow streets and numerous convents, churches and fine palaces built to house the nobility. It had also had its Moorish and Jewish quarters until the infamous decree of Expulsion in 1492 when it was said that about 30,000 Jews left Spain altogether. In Avila was located the ornate Dominican monastery of St Thomas, built to celebrate the victory over the Moors at Granada and decorated in memory of the occasion with countless intricate carvings of the pomegranate. Here the Grand Inquisitor had his headquarters for a while. Here were guarded before the high altar the first *sanbenitas* seen in Spain. Here was recounted the story of a Jew who had desecrated the Host, for which crime he and some of his co-religionists were solemnly burnt in expiation. Here officiated the Grand Inquisitor, Torquemada, said to be responsible for the decree promulgated by the Catholic Kings which expelled all Jews and Moors from the realm. Torquemada himself lies buried under a plain stone slab in the sacristy of St Thomas, a silent reminder of Spain's period of dishonour.

The recently vacated Jewish quarter of Avila offered a home to Juan Sanchez and his sons, who quickly adopted their mother's patronymic, Cepeda, and strove to erase the stain from their past. Juan wanted at least to regain a sense of human dignity and ensure a future for his family in a society where orthodoxy was a *sine qua non* of social acceptance. He forthwith saw to it that his children received a thorough Catholic education and married into reputable 'old Christian' families. Gradually the stigma of polluted blood that adhered to the 'new Christians' was overcome and the family attained to an honoured place in Catholic Avilese society.

Outwardly Spain was enjoying an unparallelled period of glory. The learning of the Renaissance, the translation of the first polyglot bible published in 1522 by Spanish scholars, the founding of the University of Alcala de Henares which rivalled Salamanca for intellectual primacy, the expansion overseas into recently discovered South America 'the Indies', all added to Spain's prestige. In Teresa's lifetime the country was enriched by the presence of universally revered saints – John of Avila, Ignatius Loyola, Francis Borgia, Peter of Alcantara, John of the Cross; her teachers, writers and explorers were known throughout Europe. But the glory was ephemeral. It was the bloom of a ripe and luscious fruit already rotten at the core. By exalting the notion of 'pure blood' and absolute orthodoxy Spain ultimately stifled her growth and undermined her whole economy and culture.

Teresa's span was the last flaming of a fire soon to be extinguished. In her, Spain and Spanish Catholicism reached a zenith before their decline. But how ironic that, instead of the pure Castilian lineage so lauded by her later biographers, Teresa had in fact sprung from a despised and marginalised people. She held within herself the seeds of a far richer culture than she cared to admit openly – the culture of a Spain that embraced many races and religious beliefs – not one alone.

Little Teresa, the newborn, black haired baby who first saw the light on that March morning of 1515 was partially at least a daughter of Israel.[2] Her independence, courage and wit vie with those of Judith and Esther, heroines of the Old Testament; and it is noteworthy that when she reached adulthood she chose to enter an Order which originated in the Holy Land and had legendary roots (in which Teresa implicitly believed) stretching back to the prophet Elijah. When she wrote in later life her theme was continually "the mercies of the Lord", just as her forebears had sung for so many years at that Passover festival which became her own Easter:

> Though our mouths were full of song as the sea,
> And our tongues of exultation as the multitude of the
>   waters,
> And our lips with praise as the expanse of the
>   firmament;
> Though our eyes were radiant like the sun and moon,
> And our hands were spread forth like the eagles
>   of heaven,
> And our feet were swift as hinds;
> We should yet be unable to thank thee
> O Lord our God and God of our ancestors,
> Even for one in a thousand
> Of the many thousands of thousands
> And myriad of myriads of kindnesses
> That thou hast wrought upon our forebears and
>   upon us.[3]

NOTES

1. *Way of Perfection*, ch. 3.
2. A full treatment of St Teresa's ancestry together with the relevant documentary evidence can be found in the article *The Historical Setting of St Teresa's Life* by Teófanes Egidio ODC in *Carmelite Studies*, vol. 1, ICS Publications 1980.
3. From the Passover Liturgy. Quoted in *Light and Rejoicing, A Christian Understanding of Jewish Worship,* by W. Simpson, Christian Journals Ltd, Belfast 1976.

A girl growing

Childhood and youth in Avila. 1515-36

By the time he was in his early twenties Alonso Sanchez de Cepeda, Teresa's father, found himself furnished with a suitable, though fictitious, ancestral pedigree and a certificate (purchased by Juan Sanchez at an exorbitant price) testifying that he was an *hidalgo* or Spanish nobleman. He had also married a bride of old Christian stock, Catalina del Peso y Heñao, who duly bore him three children.

When Catalina died prematurely Alonso further consolidated his position by obtaining a dispensation to wed her distant cousin, the beautiful fourteen year old Beatriz de Ahumada. Beatriz was to bear Alonso another nine children of which Teresa was the third. The only other girls in the immediate family were Maria, Catalina's daughter, and Juana, Beatriz'benjamin, thirteen years younger than her sister. Teresa therefore grew up in the midst of a clan of adoring brothers who were both playmates and co-conspirators in her pranks. Rather than being a demure little miss she gives the impression of a lively tomboy.

One of Teresa's early escapades (if we are to believe her first biographer) was carried out with her brother Rodrigo, four years older than herself and a great favourite. Together they discussed the heroic deaths read about in the lives of the saints and decided forthwith to seek the glory of martyrdom for themselves. One drawback of course was "having a mother and father"[1] but, nothing daunted, they set out for the country of the Moors only to be met by an uncle as they left the city. He took them back immediately to their distraught mother. Teresa (unlike her biographer) makes no claim to having tried seriously to carry out her plans. She only says she wished she *could* have found a way to do so. Maybe what a later generation attributed to inborn heroism was merely due to the over-active imagination of two children who sneaked away from home in the intensity of their play, fully intending to be back in time for the next meal! Martyrdom however continued to fascinate Teresa and many years later she was to hold it up to her sisters as an ideal attainable without the shedding of blood.

> If you have started serving God seriously the least you can offer him is your life... If you are a real religious, a real pray-er, and want to enjoy God's favours, you obviously can't afford to shy away from wanting to die for him and undergo martyrdom. Don't you realise sisters that the life of a good religious... is one long martyrdom? I say long because in comparison with those whose heads have been chopped off in a trice one can call it long, but all our lives are short, very short in some cases ...We just have got to make no account of anything that will come to an end, least of all life, for we can't count on a single day.[2]

At other times the child Teresa played 'hermits' with Rodrigo, piling up stones for eremitical cells which toppled as soon as constructed. They were spellbound by the words "for ever... for ever... for ever..." as they pondered on eternity. But these are not specially 'holy' thoughts. They highlight the usual childish delight in words and concepts outside the range of present experience. Which parent has not had a child ask "Who made me? ...and before that?... and before that?..." with the question at the end "But who made God? Who was before that?" The only game Teresa mentions as being played with other girls was the pretence of 'being nuns' and we do not need much imagination to surmise who took the part of the Mother Superior! Teresa was so loveable and loving by nature that people naturally deferred to her plans and wishes. If they did not, later events were to prove that she knew how to charm them round to her way of thinking.

Alonso was a serious and upright man, given to outward display and fine clothes to mark his hard won *hidalgo* status. He was much admired by his little girl for his tender heartedness, shown by his refusal to keep a Moorish slave as was common among others of his standing. He proved a true *paterfamilias*, his wife, children and servants revolving around him as the pivotal figure. After describing him with deep affection Teresa adds as a final accolade "He was a man of the most rigid chastity".[3] While this could merely imply that he treated his young wife honourably and did not indulge in extra-marital affairs to add a spice of romance to his life, (often lacking in a society where marriages were arranged), this trait could also account for Beatriz, who was in every respect as morally irreproachable as her husband, developing a fondness for romantic novels to fill the void left by an absence of any real conjugal partnership of love. When she died at the age of thirty-three her daughter said she already looked and dressed like a woman well advanced in years.

Doña Beatriz was pious in her gentle way, careful to see that her children learned their prayers, but she also passed on to her intelligent little daughter a guilty passion for her own reading tastes. Teresa devoured stories of romance as she grew up but was careful to hide the books from her father who, she felt sure, would not approve of such a frivolous pastime.

Teresa was thirteen when Beatriz died and, like many girls before and since, she betook herself to an image of the Blessed Virgin to implore her protection. Tearfully she knelt before one of those Spanish clothed and waxen doll-like figures and found comfort in what it symbolised – protection, warmth and motherly care. Alonso was not to marry again. One period of Teresa's life was over; henceforward she was to develop as a young woman, childhood was behind her.

* * *

Now on the threshold of adolescence, Teresa felt ready to experience some 'real life', whatever that might be. She was only a year younger than her mother had been when she married and her elder sister Maria, preparing to wed, was busy planning for her own future with Martin Guzman her betrothed. Teresa, beautiful and flirtatious, wanted to emulate the adults around her.

In the book of her *Life* she tells of how, at this crucial stage of development, she entered into a dangerous friendship. With her mother's death and her sister's preoccupation the house was left open to the visits of various cousins who otherwise would not have gained admission to the intimate family circle. They were children of her aunt Elvira, widowed sister of Alonso. One of the cousins befriended Teresa and initiated her into women's gossip and the pleasures of clothes and jewellery. She found herself drawn into the equivalent of the Avilese jet-set. Though it was all most likely relatively harmless, the strictness of her upbringing may easily have made Teresa feel more guilty than was warranted over her adolescent peccadilloes. She stresses too that she never lost her honour despite her indiscretions, nor her father's implicit trust in her goodness. He had an inkling that all was not well but did nothing to hinder his daughter's enjoyment.

Exactly what sort of relationship Teresa so bitterly reproached herself for is not clear. Many have assumed a flirtation with a young man, one of her cousins, though she does not say so herself. It is just as likely that what troubled her conscience in later life was a passionate or deeply sentimental attachment to another woman who took the impressionable girl into her confidence and to whom Teresa, deprived of a mother's love, clung in order to relieve her loneliness.

In those days too, female chastity was so strictly guarded that any unofficial 'affair' with a man would speedily have been extinguished by Don Alonso and his sons. Teresa's

20

love for her father, always tender and deep, would not permit any stain on the family's honour, or even allow the slightest suspicion of such.

However, Don Alonso was eventually roused to action, for he felt Teresa was morally endangered by her cousins' society even if technically she was innocent of serious fault. He did not wish publicly to impugn his daughter's good will but fortunately the circumstances of the moment played into his hands. With Maria recently married and in her new husband's country house some distance away it was considered unsuitable for a girl of Teresa's age to be left unchaperoned at home. Teresa too had tired of deception and intrigue. Her honest nature hated any kind of dissimulation however pleasant it might be temporarily. She was relieved when her father offered to send her to the Augustinian nuns of Our Lady of Grace where she could complete her education with daughters of the best families.

Teresa spent a restless preliminary week as a boarder, afraid her companion pupils might guess why she had been sent away from home. But when she realised no hint of scandal had tainted her good name she relaxed and settled down in her new environment.

For the nuns of Our Lady of Grace Teresa conceived a deep and abiding affection. Many years later she read Augustine's *Confessions* and admitted that she loved him so much, not only because he had been a great sinner like herself, but because she had been to school with nuns of his Order. The novice mistress Sr Maria, who was in charge of the pupils, impressed the young Teresa with her piety and goodness. Gradually, in her tranquil new environment, Teresa found her thoughts turning towards God; but although prayer now became a part of her daily life she still harboured a repugnance for the religious state. "I was still anxious not to be a nun for God had not as yet given me this desire, although I was also afraid of marriage" as she openly admitted.[4] There is certainly no proof that Teresa ever seriously considered marriage as an option. Did she not have the example of her mother before her – living in almost monastic seclusion in the Cepeda mansion, worn out from childbearing, whiling away her time reading novels, completely under the authority of her husband? In her writings Teresa encourages her own nuns to bear any hardships in their lives by contrasting *their* happy lot with that of their married sisters.

> Think too how many married women – people of position as I know, – have serious complaints and sore trials and yet dare not complain to their husbands about them for fear of annoying them. Sinner that I am! Surely we have not come here to indulge ourselves more than they! Learn to suffer a little for the love of God without telling everyone about it. When a woman has made an unhappy marriage she does not talk about it or complain of it, lest it come to her husband's knowledge; she has to endure a great deal of misery and yet has no one to whom she can relieve her mind.[5]

It seemed to Teresa she had to make a choice. What direction should she take regarding her own future?

She chatted with the younger nuns at Our Lady of Grace in an attempt to clarify her thoughts. These were probably girls around her own age, as teenage novices were common. Like marriages, religious vocations tended to be 'arranged' and no doubt some of her companions were destined to progress to the cloister when their education was finished without having any say in the matter at all. The young sisters let it be known that they felt the regime was too severe and made excessive demands on them. Teresa, being no heroine, forthwith turned her thoughts to a less strict convent, that of the Incarnation, which followed a modified Carmelite rule and where she already had a close friend, Juana Suarez. If she had to be a nun, at least let her enter a place where the life would be reasonably pleasant!

Teresa's mind toyed with the options, unable to decide finally one way or another. The indecision affected her health. She became ill with the first of many such mysterious ailments that dogged her through life. She returned to her father's house and when she had recovered sufficiently it was arranged that she should convalesce at the residence of her half-sister Maria and her husband. En route to their country home at Castellanos she stopped to spend a few days with an uncle, who in his old age became a friar, though at this point he still dwelt in his own house immersed in religious books and private devotions. He asked Teresa to read to him from his store of pious tracts and the impressionable young woman, weak from illness, was suddenly made to see how far she was from any kind of holiness. Fear gripped her. What if she had died? Where would she have been then?

For three months Teresa wrestled with her fears. At last she capitulated. Christ would have her life though she felt no natural attraction whatever towards the convent. She bolstered up her decision by reading the *Letters* of St.Jerome to sustain her courage; then she approached her father. Don Alonso was heartbroken. How could he lose his favourite daughter? Stubbornly he refused consent – Teresa would go only over his dead body! Equally stubborn about getting her own way she took her brother Antonio into her confidence. One November night they set out secretly together. This time it was not a game of projected martyrdom but the start of her very personal way of the cross. She tells of the decisive event in her inimitable manner.

> I remember – and really believe it to be true – that when I left my father's house so great was my distress that I do not think it will be greater when I die. It seemed to me as if every bone in my body was being wrenched asunder... But the Lord gave me courage to fight myself and so I carried out my intention.[6]

Antonio left Teresa at the Convent of the Incarnation and himself proceeded to the monastery of St Thomas. Don Alonso lost two children at once. Behind them the doors were shut and they were taken to the heart of their respective communities.

So ended Teresa's adolescence. The young woman of twenty-one had made her decision and would stick by it. It was her first victory.

NOTES

1. *Life*, ch. 1.
2. *Way of Perfection*, ch. 12 (Kavanaugh translation).
3. *Life*, ch. 1.
4. Ibid., ch. 3.
5. *Way of Perfection*, ch. 11.
6. *Life*, ch. 3.

Sub umbra Carmeli

The year of noviciate. November 1536-37

In those days there was no preliminary period of probation before the habit was received. Teresa, on her entry into the convent was immediately clothed with the brown tunic, scapular, white veil and mantle of a Carmelite novice – suitably modelled of course and of fine material befitting a daughter of Don Alonso (all her life Teresa was fastidious about her cleanliness and attire). Thus divested of her secular dress and looking the part of a young nun, suddenly and radiantly happy at having accomplished her plans, she went to the parlour to greet her father who had been summarily sent for on the morrow.

Faced with a *fait accompli* and secretly proud of his daughter's spirit, Don Alonso accepted the inevitable and gave the runaway his blessing. After all, his Teresa was still living in Avila, close enough for frequent visits. The life she had chosen was no disgrace and she was in congenial society. He went away from the convent comforted.

Teresa was now set to begin her year of Noviciate. What manner of Order had she entered almost by chance – an Order she was destined to reform so brilliantly a quarter of a century later that her name and that of Carmel are forever linked?

The Carmelite Order traces its origin to a group of hermits who settled on Mount Carmel in Palestine during the period of the crusades. There they established a *laura* or number of small single cells, and later built a chapel dedicated to the Blessed Virgin whom, in typical feudal fashion they recognised as their 'lady' while Christ was their leige-Lord. At that time the hermit life was everywhere undergoing a revival, a popular reaction against the wealth and landed security of the great monastic establishments. There was a general desire for a more personal following of Jesus in prayer, poverty and single-heartedness. The hermits of Mount Carmel, who were composed of retired crusaders and pilgrims to the holy places, asked for and received a Rule from the then Latin Patriarch of Jerusalem, Albert Avogadro, sometime between 1206 and 1214. Albert was a career churchman, prominent in diplomatic affairs, who had been a canon regular of the Holy Cross at Mortara. His life was brought to an unexpectedly violent end in 1214 when he was assassinated (during a procession) by the former Master of the Hospital of the Holy Spirit, whom he had deposed and publicly rebuked for immorality. As a canon Albert had himself followed the Rule of St Augustine and he had later been on the commission which compiled a Rule for the Humiliati. The *regula vitae*, or form of life he gave to the hermits reflects his own background, and in the Carmelite Order he is honoured as St Albert, though he is not venerated among the Augustinians. Albert's Rule is scripturally based, setting forth a simple lifestyle and emphasising solitude and continual prayer. One hermit, B. is addressed as prior; the hermits are all brothers and are to elect their own leader to whom they must promise obedience and who has the duty of guarding the enclosure. From their location on Mount Carmel the group obviously looked to Elijah as their inspiration and patron, and the Order has always stressed a prophetic as well as a contemplative dimension.

When the Holy Land was retaken by the Saracens the hermits dispersed to their countries of origin. Some came to England as early as 1242; others went to Cyprus, others to France and Italy. But with their unusual striped cloaks, *carpeta* (which legend says originated from the scorch marks left on Elijah's mantle as he let it fall from the fiery chariot) and oriental customs, they found it hard to establish themselves. The Carthusians were flourishing – why then another Order of hermits of whom people knew nothing and who had no means of attracting vocations?

In Europe therefore the Rule was adapted to meet the changed circumstances in which the hermits found themselves. The purely eremitical vocation ceased to be followed by the majority of men and they came to take their place in the mediaeval church as one of the mendicant Orders. A white mantle replaced the much maligned *carpeta* and Carmelites taught and studied in the universities beside their Franciscan and Dominican counterparts. The ideal of single cell living and continual prayer receded further and further from their consciousness as the friars became involved in academic and pastoral work, though the Order's origins were never completely disregarded and the prophetic ideal continued to inspire and attract newcomers. After the Black Death with its accompanying ravages further modifications were made in the Rule and discipline relaxed on many counts. Suffice to point out that Fra Filippo Lippi (1404-69) the Florentine Carmelite and renaissance painter was notorious for his immoral life though his pictures are full of the tenderest piety. A variety of reform movements recalled Carmelites to their first fervour, but the Order lacked strong leadership and a real sense of purpose. The transition to mendicancy had not been wholly successful. The Spanish friars, cut off from the rest of their European brethren, remained untouched by currents of reform and continued along their own way, fiercely independent.

At first a female branch of the Order was not envisaged. However, with the growth of the béguine movement and the hierarchy's insistence that those women who wished to live dedicated lives outside the traditional monastic structures should align themselves to recognised Orders, some did indeed come under Carmelite influence. Béguines tended to choose association with one of the mendicant groups because of their relative freedom from monastic discipline and their tendency towards a deeply personal popular piety.

In 1452 John Soreth, Prior General of the Carmelites, wrote a set of Constitutions for some béguine communities of the Netherlands who wished to join the Order. The legislation stressed prayer, solitude and the common life; but other convents, especially in Italy, continued with a variety of lifestyles, just changing their official status from béguines (or *mantellatae*) to nuns. Perhaps the only thing that linked them to the Order were the traditional vows of the mendicants (poverty, chastity and obedience rather than the Benedictine vows of stability, obedience and the conversion of manners), a love for the blessed Virgin (always strong in Carmel) and a collection of legends, stretching back to the prophet Elijah, which endeavoured to provide prestige for an Order that otherwise seemed rather insignificant.

The Convent of the Incarnation which Teresa entered on 2 November 1535 had begun, like many similar establishments, as a *beatorio* (the Spanish equivalent of a béguinage). Founded at the end of the fifteenth century it was later incorporated into the Carmelite Order, and friars in the town undertook the direction of the women according to their Order's spirituality. The community in due course established itself in a sprawling farmhouse-type building outside the walls of Avila on the site of the old Jewish cemetery, the first Mass being offered there, as already remarked, on the very day Teresa was baptised. She did not therefore enter into a well established monastery with a long and venerable tradition, but one still struggling for an identity and not being very successful in the process.

Although it had originated as a poor convent (*beatorios* tended to cater for the merchant class rather than for the aristocracy) the Incarnation soon housed daughters of local *hidalgos*. It was a useful retreat for young girls lacking sufficient dowry for a good match, or for widows who wished to end their days in peace. The place, aristocratic in tone, knew real poverty. In winter it was reported that snow blew into the choir and settled on the habits of the nuns as they sang the Office. The Incarnation met a genuine social, rather than religious need, and numbers increased accord-

28

ingly until, at the time of Teresa's entry there were one hundred and thirty women, a large community by any standards. The poorer sisters slept in a common dormitory, worked hard in the house and garden and often went hungry owing to lack of communal funds. Those who came from wealthy homes were provided with a suite of rooms and received an allowance from their kinsfolk to cover expenses of a personal nature. The sisters were quite happy for some of their number to spend intervals away from the convent. This relieved the financial situation as hosts would supply visiting nuns with food and other provisions. It was all haphazard in the extreme, ruinous of sisterly equality and religious discipline.

Teresa does not seem to have seen anything untoward in those early days as she contemplated the conventual arrangements; only later did she realise how the structures had hindered rather than helped her. Don Alonso on disposing of her dowry saw to it that his daughter had fitting accommodation. She was given a private apartment comprising guestroom, bedroom, kitchen and oratory. The oratory became one of Teresa's favourite places and she loved to keep it clean and beautifully decorated for her devotions. As to her fellow nuns, it would be impossible to say whether or not the majority were called to religious life or whether they were there merely for family reasons. Many seem to have been frustrated at their lack of freedom and sought to evade any sacrifice; others were truly loving and sacrificial but lacked the firm direction that would have helped them to put their better impulses into action.

It is difficult to conjecture what kind of formation the Convent of the Incarnation could offer the young Doña Teresa de Ahumada during her year of noviciate. She says nothing of her novice mistress or fellow novices so we have no real means of knowing the type of instruction offered. *The Book of the Institution of the First Monks* purporting to be a much earlier work than the fourteenth century which produced it, was almost certainly in use as a text of Carmelite spiritual teaching and there must also have been lives of the saints and collections of legends. Teresa continued to hold these dear – such as the story that St Anne and St Merentiana (our Lady's mother and grandmother respectively) had taken the child Mary to visit the successors of Elijah living in solitude on Mount Carmel and that later Mary and the apostles had become members of the Order! We might smile at this today but we have to remember that historical research as we understand it was virtually non-existent; edification was considered more important than literal truth. From her early days too Teresa vaguely understood Carmel as being (as indeed it was) an Order dedicated to prayer on account of its eremitical beginnings, but as yet she had little idea of how to tackle this aspect of her vocation.

Her noviciate was basically happy. The joy of being in the habit, all indecision behind her, endowed her with inner peace and a sense of freedom which was never to leave her. She had no regrets. Her character remained the same – she did not like to do anything which made her look ridiculous, she hated any form of correction or occasions when her lack of experience showed up – but her gaiety took on a softer aspect and did not preclude seriousness when appropriate. She began to think things out for herself, to meditate on life's shortness and to learn from good example when she saw it as the following incident reveals:

> At that time there was a nun who was afflicted by a most serious and painful illness: she was suffering from open sores in the stomach which had been caused by obstructions and these forced her to reject all food. Of this illness she soon died. I saw all the nuns were afraid of it but for my own part I had only great envy at her patience. I begged God that he would send me any illness he pleased if only he would make me as patient as she.[1]

Teresa overcame her natural fastidiousness and she nursed this nun until she died. She had a genuine care for others.

Apart from this spell of nursing Teresa was occupied in simple household tasks, instructions in the religious life from her novice mistress and learning to follow the books needed for Divine Office in choir. Her employments were consonant with her social standing; life was pleasant, her companions congenial, and she was not required to do anything excessive in the way of penance or mortification. Had she not offered to care for the repulsively sick nun no-one would have dreamed of asking her to do so. Yet there was still a restlessness beneath the surface. Had she broken free of home and family just to find another equally pleasant and congenial environment behind the honey-coloured walls of the Incarnation?

Teresa was resolved to go forward and "give everything" whatever that might mean. At the end of her first year she made her vows with great resolution – she was bound to Christ forever. She passed through the rows of sisters, all in new white linen toques provided by Don Alonso as part of his daughter's dowry, and all sat down after the ceremony to a festive meal, Teresa resplendent in the black veil of her vows. Her cup of happiness was overflowing. She was a fully-fledged nun!

NOTE

1. *Life*, ch. 5.

The discovery of prayer

Illness and the influence of Osuna. 1538-42

Not long after her profession Teresa's health began to deteriorate. The change in diet and lifestyle affected her adversely and ailments, including fainting fits and palpitations, became so frequent as to cause alarm.

Don Alonso, filled with concern, arranged for the best doctors of Avila to treat his daughter but to no avail. It seemed that the recently consecrated young nun would have to leave her convent and seek a cure further afield. At least, as Teresa wryly remarks, she could not "offend God"[1] in her present state of health. Indeed it may be that the natural exuberance of her temperament and the lack of any real challenge in the life she had chosen combined to make her unconsciously seek relief in sickness. She had admired the heroism of the old nun she had nursed; perhaps in illness she too could rise to sanctity and obtain virtues that seemed denied to the more robust, beset as they were with temptations on every side.

It is worth noting that, while Teresa never enjoyed good health in her own estimation, she overcame her inherent weakness in middle-age and accomplished the foundation of convents all over Castile, displaying the energy of a vigorous woman many years younger. She would stay up all night cleaning and preparing a convent or write business letters well past the time when all others were in bed. However, at the Incarnation she was in the position of a woman insufficiently challenged, her capacities untapped. These turned inwards and wreaked havoc on her body.

As the doctors summoned by Don Alonso pronounced their bafflement at her symptoms, Teresa decided to take advantage of her half-sister Maria's offer of hospitality at her Castellanos house. Maria had discovered a *currendera* who lived at nearby Becedas and had a great reputation for healing. She might be a regular 'old wife' with her magical remedies but it seemed Teresa's only hope. She and her friend Juana Suarez left the Incarnation to travel to Maria's home and, as before, Teresa broke her journey to visit her Uncle Pedro. He lent her a book called *The Third Spiritual Alphabet* by Francis de Osuna, in which the Franciscan described a manner of recollecting oneself and practising mental prayer.

While she waited for spring and the *currendera* to begin treatment Teresa rested and reflected and read her new book. For her it was a tremendous discovery. There *was* a way of prayer but it demanded work, effort, method. Here was the challenge and direction she had been unconsciously seeking. Teresa was never a woman to minimise the basic foundation necessary for praying – guard of the heart, a disciplined life, great purity of conscience, a growing love for the person of the Saviour. Osuna's book set her on the path she was henceforth to follow, though experience led her to modify in her own teaching his 'angelic' approach and place greater emphasis on Christ the Man, who can never be disregarded even at the highest levels of contemplation.

Osuna bases his theory on a manner of prayer which starts with 'recollecting' the senses, entering within, and detaching oneself from transient things. It was all new to the nun who, reclining at her sister's country home, away from conventual routine and the daily round of vocal prayer in choir, sat viewing the forested countryside so different to Avila's stony plains and realised that a personal relationship with God was offered to her. In her Order, ostensibly dedicated to prayer, it began to dawn on her that more was involved in that than she had dreamed. With Osuna for her guide she set foot on the path of contemplation. Almost immediately Teresa experienced in her life some of the effects of seriously trying to pray, God granted her what she terms the 'prayer of quiet' an ability to rest peacefully in his presence, and even briefly the 'prayer of Union'. She developed a method of imagining Christ within her. This she described in the *Way of Perfection* which she later wrote to help her own nuns take the first steps in prayer.

> Imagine this Lord himself is at your side and see how lovingly and humbly he is teaching you – and, believe me, you should stay with so good a Friend for as long as you can before you leave him. If you become accustomed to having him at your side, and if he sees that you love him to be there and are always trying to please him, you will never be able, as we put it, to send him away, nor will he ever fail you ... I am not asking you now to think of him ... or to make long and subtle meditations with your understanding. I am asking you only to look at him... If you want him you will find him.[2]

Another favourite manner of meditation was to place herself in spirit beside Christ in Gethsemane, or at his feet with Mary Magdalen.[3] Teresa in this way involved her senses and her whole person as she endeavoured to activate her faith in the Lord's presence.

She had more difficulty in harnessing her thoughts to discursive meditation, and from the style of her writing it is obvious that her train of reasoning tended to go off on a tangent. She supplemented this deficiency by reading good books, pausing frequently to think over what she had read. For eighteen years she admits she could not even *begin* to pray unless she had a book on hand[4] – she was no 'natural' mystic! As a beginner she was humble enough to do what she could, not striving for the heights before laying a strong foundation. Knowledge was, she saw, indispensible for a properly balanced piety. Love needs something, and above all Someone, to lean on. Teresa appreciated the human need for reading and reflection and did not make the mistake of thinking that love can develop in a vacuum. Trial and error enabled her to find what suited her best, so that many years before Dom John Chapman of Downside she was living by his famous dictum "Pray as you can, not as you can't". Yet despite her best efforts Teresa had not fully mastered her will. Her conscience was insufficiently purified and when life and prayer are not yet yoked together there is bound to be strain and uneasiness as she was soon to discover. But meanwhile, in her solitary retreat she was relaxed and tranquil.

Wanting to find a director to hear her confession and talk of the topics that were interesting her in Osuna's book, Teresa contacted the local priest. He was a man of some learning who quickly grew fond of the eager neophyte. Their mutual friendship encouraged confidences. Teresa, genuinely interested in others and gifted with charm and insight, discovered that this new friend of hers was living in concubinage. She artlessly remarks that the woman concerned had induced the priest to wear a little charm as a memento to keep her constantly in mind. In the course of a conversation Teresa persuaded the priest to give her the mascot which she immediately got someone to throw in the river. It seems this act changed the man's heart. His love for Teresa overcame his illicit attachment, and being loved in return truly and chastely he was enabled to change his lifestyle – much to her satisfaction as he died a year later.

In her assessment of this relationship Teresa appears ambivalent. She obviously loved the priest but felt bound to express regrets at the relationship between them not being as disinterested as it might have been. She forgets in retrospect that most relationships do perforce begin imperfectly and that God uses these imperfect conditions for accomplishing his own designs. There can therefore be no real cause for self-recriminations, for if we all waited until relationships were perfectly ordered before embarking on any sort of intimacy with others most of us would never even begin. In fact, right to the end of her life all Teresa's friendships, as seen through her letters, had a strong human and emotional element. She was unable to relate as a 'good nun', only as *this* particular woman, Teresa, to this or that particular person with their strong and weak points, their unique character and gifts. If she had any outstanding gift herself it was the gift of friendship, with all its attendant risks and rewards.

Thus Teresa passed her time of waiting at Castellanos until spring when she submitted herself to the *currendera*. The treatment was drastic! Teresa mentions daily purgatives and other barbarous ministrations which she forbears to describe in detail. The result?

> At the end of two months the severity of the remedies had almost ended my life, and the pain in the heart, which I had gone there to get treated, was much worse; sometimes I felt as if sharp teeth had hold of me, and so severe was the pain they caused that it was feared I was going mad. My strength suffered a grave decline for I could take nothing but liquid, had a great distaste for food, was in continual fever, and became so wasted away that ... my nerves began to shrink. These symptoms were accompanied by intolerable pain which gave me no rest by night or by day.[5]

Don Alonso, seeing the pitiable state of his favourite child took her to his home where she could be cared for in familiar surroundings. Around 15 August, feast of the Assumption, Teresa still in great pain wanted to make her confession. Her father, afraid she was imagining herself close to death, refused the request. Great was his anguish when Teresa then fell into a catatonic state which lasted four days. She was expected to die at any moment. Nuns from the Incarnation came to keep vigil at her bedside; her grave was dug and one house of the Order, receiving news that she had already expired, actually celebrated a Requiem Mass. But Teresa did not die. She regained consciousness to find her Carmelite sisters beside her, her eyes heavy with wax, her tongue bitten to pieces.

Though death had eluded her Teresa was still far from well and would continue thus for a long time. She returned to the Incarnation paralysed and helpless. It was to be three years before her limbs returned to normal. It is good to recall here that, whatever may have been the shortcomings of the community, the sisters welcomed her back into their midst and nursed her with devoted care.

During these years of illness all Teresa had learned from Osuna's book she tried to put into practice. She yearned for time alone with God and was happy to speak of him and of the benefits of prayer when occasion arose. She also became more aware of how she had failed him in the past. A deep contrition took root in her heart coupled with self-distrust.

Gradually the nuns realised that the Doña Teresa who had returned from Castellanos was not the one who had left the Incarnation. Illness had matured her, made her adopt a more serious stand as regards the obligations of religious life. They grew to admire the young nun, still suffering physically yet strong in spirit. At this time too she developed a devotion to St Joseph which became a hallmark of her spiritual life; she was to dedicate her first convent to him and no one did more than Teresa to have this formerly neglected saint given an honoured place in the Church. She paid the expenses of St Joseph's yearly festival at the Incarnation and decorated her own oratory for it as well. She took him as guide and companion,[6] admiring his humble devotedness to Mary and Jesus. To his intercession she attributed the final cure of her paralysis.

As she regained her physical strength Teresa felt reborn from the dead. All she needed to do now was to set her course and steer straight forward – or so it seemed.

NOTES

1. *Life*, ch. 4.
2. *Way of Perfection*, ch. 26
3. *Life*, ch. 8.
4. *Life*, ch. 4.
5. *Life*, ch. 5.
6. Cf *Life*, ch. 6.

The path of conversion

Struggling between two worlds. 1542-54

Had Teresa been a married woman she would, in her late twenties, have been worn out from child-bearing and well on the way to a dowdy middle-age. Instead at twenty-seven she was at the apex of youthful maturity, vital and beautiful with sparkling black eyes and clear Castilian skin. Her attractiveness was enhanced by a line of three small moles which added piquancy to her face. Her mouth was described as small, her nose straight and well-formed. We can picture easily enough how a pleasant appearance wedded to inner virtue and sincerity caused people to be drawn to this nun, her purity being made accessible by a manner both warm and compassionate. Besides, she was acknowledged as a proficient pray-er and she enjoyed her burgeoning role of mentor to the uninitiated. Already she was something of a celebrity and she revelled in it; she would have been less than human otherwise – and such she never was!

The parlours of the Incarnation were equivalent to society salons in Teresa's day. Men and women from the town came regularly to see family and friends, flirtations were not unknown and there was a great deal of merry chatter and social gossip. Teresa had relations to talk with her in her suite of rooms, others crowded the parlour to hear her discourse on prayer according to Osuna's method and to learn from her how to make a meditation. One of her first disciples was her own rapidly aging father. Don Alonso, with the thought of heaven and hell uppermost in his mind, was determined to secure a place in the former. He humbly followed his daughter's instructions until he actually found talking about prayer a waste of time. He came less and less to the parlour and spent longer periods at his orisons. By this time Teresa had almost abandoned prayer herself. Her conscience was smitten.

Teresa meant well. She had received many graces from the Lord and wished to pass on her knowledge to others and thus encourage them to pray, but she was very much at the mercy of her emotions, lacking in discretion and self-discipline. Also, the structures of the convent were not supportive. It was taken for granted that she would be available for family and friends, that she would give spiritual instruction, would talk to benefactors who provided the Incarnation with much needed revenue. Serious or prolonged recollection seemed out of the question. Yet even with all this talking Teresa never allowed herself to speak ill of anyone; in her presence there was no malicious back-biting, no sarcastic wit, no insinuations. With her, anyone absent from the group knew their reputation to be safe. This in itself is a remarkable achievement and the fruit of grace, for Teresa could easily have drawn an admiring clique around herself at others' expense. To control one's tongue is a proof of real maturity, and though Teresa speaks lightly of this achievement it should not deceive us into thinking she was such a 'beginner' as she makes out.

However, as her social life expanded the life of prayer and effort began to pall. Teresa certainly loved God, but surely there was still very much to enjoy apart from his company! She spoke of prayer but only prayed sporadically. She was utterly torn between total self-giving and her other friendships which included plenty of frivolity and the personal admiration accorded her by her devotees. Her happiness was never unmarred. When at prayer she longed for the sands to run down and the hour to be over so that she could hasten to the parlour. When with her visitors she was tormented by the thought of what she owed God and was not giving him. She was trying to serve two masters while receiving full payment from neither.

In her vacillation Teresa took up another intimate but anonymous friendship, which taxed her emotionally and held her in its grip; though as usual she gives no explicit details except to say that she seemed incapable of making a break despite two clear warnings. One was a vision of Christ looking displeased – a look of sad reproach which she remembered for many years; the other was when a toad, symbol of evil, crossed the parlour pavingstones as she was conversing with her visitor. But by this time Teresa was unable to help herself; the spirit was willing, the flesh weak. Prayer was a torment for she knew that, taken seriously, it would mean having to remedy her ways. She was still young, attractive – why forego earthly joys when she had no assurance of heavenly ones? And anyway, she was not behaving in such a manner as was considered sinful, nor did she compromise her honour in the slightest. Outwardly she was a zealous and observant nun. Everyone said as much, except an older relative, also a member of the Incarnation, who warned her of laxity. Teresa felt the nun was just being scrupulous and disregarded the proferred advice.

In 1549 Don Alonso died. Teresa went home to nurse him during his last illness and marvelled at how close he had grown to God. Witnessing his final agony she felt an overwhelming grief which she resolutely concealed. In him she was losing the dearest person on earth and Teresa never rose above a genuine and deep human love for members of her family. The guilty secret of their origins had made them stand together against outside intrusion, and when Alonso was buried after a most Christian death Teresa took her young sister Juana to live with her in the guestroom of her apartment at the convent until she should find a suitable husband.

In the aftermath of sorrow Teresa bared her soul to her father's confessor, the Dominican priest Vincent Barron. He encouraged her to go regularly to Communion and resume the practice of prayer. This she did, though without sufficient resolution to really amend her life.

Twenty years were to pass; years of fluctuation between loving God and trying to reconcile this with her sociable instincts. Interiorly Teresa was worn out from the struggle. She could not integrate these two equally God-given sides of her nature however much she tried. A miracle of grace would be needed, a direct gift from God to effect the final transformation.

The watershed came one day in an unexpected manner. The love of Christ was about to supercede all other loves in her heart and lead her to the integration she had tried in vain to achieve by herself. She had done what she could, now in Christ she would discover a new and deeper union with all whom she held dear. For this, the decisive meeting with Jesus was of paramount importance. It was a meeting she never forgot.

Weary of soul at her long-standing lukewarmness she happened to go one day into the oratory. There her eyes lighted on an image of the wounded Christ which had been left in readiness for some approaching festival and which bore the realistic and bloody appearance so typical of Spanish devotional art. Teresa, gazing at such a representation of the Saviour was overwhelmed by a sense of her own sinfulness:

> So great was my distress when I thought how ill I had repaid him for those wounds that I felt my heart was breaking, and I threw myself down beside him, shedding floods of tears and begging him to give me strength once for all so that I might not offend him... When I saw that image of which I am speaking, I think I must have made greater progress, because I had quite lost trust in myself and was placing all my confidence in God. I believe I told him I would not rise from that spot until he had granted me what I was beseeching of him. And I feel sure that this did me good, for from that time onwards I began to improve.[1]

Thus began the period of serious conversion, a period of intensified prayer, recollection and reading (she was especially influenced by the *Confessions* of St Augustine). She had come through what she was later to describe in the Fifth Mansion of her *Interior Castle*. The crysallis had begun to find the freedom of the butterfly.

This is one of Teresa's most striking metaphors and it would be well to dwell on it here for a while. She had always loved nature and found it an excellent way of entering into prayer; the very sight of fields, water, plants, roused in her an intimation of the Creator's magnificence. When therefore she was told about the life cycle of the silkworm her imagination was soon at work. She ruminated on how the grubs feed on mulberry leaves until they are full grown, whereupon they spin a cocoon of silk around themselves and "die" within it. From the cocoon emerges in due course not the worm that went in but a beautiful white butterfly. Here, Teresa says, is a symbol of our own lives. Spiritually we are as a tiny grub which has to grow by nourishing itself on the mulberry leaves of good reading and meditation. When sufficiently developed it starts to spin its cocoon, enwrapping itself in silk to be "hidden with Christ in God". Spinning the cocoon comprises the renunciation of self-love in its various forms: putting others first, doing our ordinary duties well, practising prayer, obedience, mortification ... in other words doing all *we* can do. The transformation into the butterfly which follows is *God's* work. He will take our poor efforts and unite them with his Divine strength. Thus we are brought to resurrection – life in him.[2]

So begins a new way of living even here below. It is a life given wholly to God. Teresa was to live this life henceforth with all its outward ups and downs, but inwardly she was radically changed. She was, as in another image she uses, as wax imprinted with God's seal.[3] He had indeed sealed her for his own many years ago when she first embarked on the spiritual path at Castellanos. Now she was to become his living ikon – Teresa of Jesus. Well could she exclaim with joy at knowing herself to be so loved, so graced:

I have often reflected with amazement upon God's great goodness and my soul has delighted in the thought of his great magnificence and mercy. May he be blessed for all this, for it has become clear to me that, even in this life, he has not failed to reward me for any of my good desires. However wretched and imperfect my good works have been, this Lord of mine has been improving them, perfecting them and making them of greater worth, and yet hiding my evil deeds and my sins as soon as they have been committed. He has even allowed the eyes of those who have seen them to be blind to them, and he blots them from their memory. He gilds my faults and makes some virtue of mine to shine forth in splendour; yet it was he himself who gave it me and almost forced me to possess it.[4]

NOTES

1. *Life*, ch. 9.
2. Cf *Interior Castle*, Mansion 5, ch. 2.
3. Ibid.
4. *Life*, ch. 4.

With Christ as my life

Gaining the victory 1554-56

The floodgates being opened Teresa rapidly advanced along a way of mystical 'favours' – locutions, visions, raptures, in which the man Jesus figures prominently. She 'hears' him speaking to her interiorly, 'sees' his divine hands, his face, his resurrected body in all its glory.[1] She intuits the motions of his heart, and this is climaxed by a mystical wounding of her own heart from the fiery dart of a seraph. She describes her visions with a baroque flourish coupled with deep sincerity:

> Almost invariably the Lord showed himself to me in his resurrection body... Only occasionally, to strengthen me when I was in tribulation, did he show me his wounds, and then he would appear sometimes as he was on the cross and sometimes as he was in the garden... Sometimes I see him looking at me compassionately and his gaze has such power that my soul cannot endure it and remains in so sublime a rapture that it loses this beauteous vision in order to have the greater fruition of it all.[2]

We cannot doubt that at this period of her spiritual journey Jesus became Teresa's centre-point, the focus of her ardent temperament. She as a whole woman-person aligned herself irrevocably on the side of Christ emotionally, spiritually, psychically.

What today can we make of all this? First of all I think we have to acknowledge that much of what Teresa records is due to the fact that she had little formal education; her reading was limited, the Scriptures in the vernacular were banned. Unlike her male counterpart John of the Cross who had a thorough theological grounding her imagination was perforce fed upon the images and pictures which decorated the Spanish churches of the Renaissance. Several times she says she saw Christ or the Virgin 'as depicted' in a certain painting with which she was familiar. Also, while carefully explaining the difference between certain types of visions and locutions in a semi-scientific manner she never encouraged these paranormal manifestations in her nuns and maintained a healthy scepticism about their origins. On the basis of her observation of others she was convinced that supernatural phenomena could be the result of psychic weakness. There was always more certainty in love of neighbour, progress in selflessness and an increase in virtue. Even so, Teresa implicitly believed in all *she* heard and saw, and through these phenomena attained a high degree of mystical prayer.

The test of genuine prayer is the fruit it bears in life. Teresa was a woman of passion and she developed a passionate love that went out to Christ in himself and Christ in others. She was no self-centred introvert. The type of woman Teresa mistrusted was the one turned in upon self, especially if she showed signs of abnormal mystical experience. "They call it rapture. I call it nonsense!" she says tartly of nuns who behave in this way while thinking that natural psychic weakness is a sign of great spirituality. Such people need to be given plenty of work to take their minds off themselves and have formal prayer time curtailed until they are more sensible.[3]

For me, one very revealing description of Teresa's own inner pilgrimage is that which she gives when she declares that she saw the place prepared for her in hell:

...The entrance, I thought, resembled a very long, narrow passage, like a furnace, very low and dark and closely confined. The ground seemed to be full of water which looked like filthy, evil smelling mud, and in it were many wicked looking reptiles. At the end there was a hollow place scooped out of the wall like a cupboard and it was here that I found myself in close confinement... In that pestilential spot, where I was quite powerless to hope for comfort, it was impossible to sit or lie... There was no light and everything was in blackest darkness.[4]

Does not this sound like a modern psychologist's description of someone reliving the birth trauma? Teresa ostensibly was struggling for a true rebirth, substituting the centrality of Christ for the centrality of self-gratification. She was reliving in its totality the meaning of fundamental conversion. Others had 'visions' and heard 'voices' just as she did. Several were penanced by the Inquisition; a few are names which figure briefly in the pages of religious history – Juana de la Cruz, Magdalena de la Cruz... Teresa alone shines through the dimness, her spirit radiant and serene, her feet firmly planted on this earth.

Much of Teresa's spiritual progress can be attributed to her sound common sense and acceptance of the human condition. She eschewed any kind of angelism and rooted herself firmly as a person in relationship with the Person of Jesus (friend of saints and sinners alike), and in the mainstream of Catholic tradition. In the sixth mansion of the *Interior Castle* where Teresa describes the locutions and visions of one approaching close union with God she admits that she is writing autobiographically. She charts *her* way, the effect on *her* emotions and temperament. But the most important chapter of the Sixth Mansion is not one of those devoted to mystical phenomena but to the humanity of Christ. It is in this we find the key to Teresian spirituality. Here she is a sure guide. Only with Christ do we find the way, for he *is* the Way. There is no other path to union with God.[6] Teresa's *Life* as she wrote it can in fact be divided into two parts. The first part of the book is her search for Christ, culminating in her conversion before the image of him as the wounded Saviour. The remainder of her story recounts how he made her fully his own.

Teresa makes a long digression at mid-point in her *Life*

to describe the stages of prayer under the allegory of four methods of watering a garden: water taken from a well, water raised by engine and buckets, water from a stream or brook, and water from heaven. Teresa returns many times to the image of water, for in the Spain of her era water was as constant a preoccupation as it had been in Palestine during our Lord's life. The burning, relentless Spanish sun needed to be complemented by rainfall, and in making her foundations Teresa was constantly obsessed by the question "Is there a well?" or "Where can the sisters get water?" for if no source was found they would have to move elsewhere. In her longing for rain Teresa discerned the image of the soul receiving all from God, and in the arduous task of drawing up water from wells the symbol of the labour of prayer when we have to do all we can to co-operate with the Giver of all gifts. In this respect she specially loved the Gospel incident of the woman of Samaria:[7]

> I call to remembrance – oh, how often – that living water of which our Lord spoke to the Samaritan woman. That Gospel had a great attraction for me; and indeed so it had even when I was a child, though I did not understand it then as I do now. I used to pray much for that living water; and I had always a picture of it representing our Lord at the well with the inscription "Domine da mihi aquam".[8]

The woman who wrote these words had progressed fro.n the flighty young person, who first brought this picture to the convent at the age of twenty-one, to a mature pray-er who had drunk of the living water of the Spirit and was as eager as her biblical counterpart to share her discovery with others. She could make her own this continuous cry:

> O Life, giving life to all! do not deny me that living water which you promised to all who long for it. I thirst for it Lord, I beg for it. I come to you![9]

The one who asks for living water receives it. Teresa was to become a proof of that Gospel promise.

As she looked back on her childhood, youth and young womanhood Teresa learned to accept all in the light of faith, integrate everything into the whole pattern of her life. We might have expected her to hide the weak areas of herself and concentrate only on the more positive graces she received. Yet for her *all* was positive. There were no wasted years. She discerned the Lord's presence in everything that had happened to her, even those events in which ostensibly he seemed to play no part: her girlhood flirtation, her procrastination in giving herself wholeheartedly, her years of illness, her lukewarmness... She realised that her life experiences had made her the unique woman she was. She could draw profit from all, like the biblical scribe bringing things new and old out of his store of treasures.[10] In her particular environment she learned to choose God because in and through everything he had chosen her. She never minimised her mistakes and infidelities but she saw them in true proportion. God, not Teresa, was the important One and he could deal with what, humanly speaking, might seem insuperable obstacles.

Here then is the basis for prayer – absolute trust – not in the abstract but in the concrete situations of each one's life. The past is past, but it can be transformed and transcended in the present if only we fix our eyes on Jesus the Saviour. Prayer and life are interwoven and in prayer we discover the meaning of life. Teresa, tossed back and forth as she had been by her character, her situation and her struggles with temptation, held fast to prayer and emerged victorious. Therefore she speaks with authority when she writes:

If a soul perseveres in spite of sins, temptations and relapses... our Lord will bring it at last – I am certain of it – to the harbour of salvation as he has brought me myself... I may speak of that which I know through experience; and so I say, let (a person) never cease from prayer, be his life ever so wicked; for prayer is the way

48

to amend it... Herein is nothing to be afraid of but everything to hope for.[11]

And she puts her finger on our main weakness. It is lack of trust in God which hinders progress more than anything else:

I used to pray to our Lord for help; but as it now seems to me I must have committed the fault of not having put my whole trust in His Majesty and so not thoroughly distrusting myself... I did not understand how all is of little profit if we do not root out all confidence in ourselves and place it wholly in God.[12]

After her definitive encounter with Christ Teresa gave herself to him in a spirit of total trust. She really let her prayer overflow into her life, determined to keep the Lord company and forget herself. She had fought a lonely battle and gained the victory. Holding nothing back she speedily matured, becoming the full woman that until then had existed only in embryo. She knew she had been permitted to drink of the living water promised by the Lord and thus her life became fuller and more Christlike as her future unfolded.

NOTES

1. *Life*, ch. 28.
2. *Life*, ch. 29.
3. *Foundations*, ch. 6
4. *Life*, ch. 32.
5. Cf *Life*, ch. 22.
6. Cf *Interior Castle*, Mansion 6. ch. 6.
7. Jn 4:1-42.
8. *Life*, ch. 30.
9. *Exclamations*.
10. Mat 13:51.
11. *Life*, ch. 8.
12. Ibid.

The seed of an idea

Spiritual advice and a new project envisioned.
1556-58

Teresa now felt the need of an experienced person who would help her evaluate the state of her soul, for Christ seemed to fill the horizon and make more and more demands on her self-giving. She wanted light to see more and strength to give more. One who appreciated as she did the doctrine of the mystical body was well aware of the dangers of 'going it alone':

> When one of you is striving after perfection, she will at once be told that she has no need to know (God's friends) – that it is enough for her to have God. But to get to know God's friends is a very good way of 'having' him; as I have discovered from experience, it is most helpful. For, under the Lord, I owe it to such persons that I am not in hell; I was always very fond of asking them to commend me to God, and so I prevailed upon them to do so.[1]

Teresa wanted help, comfort and guidance. She looked around for trustworthy counsellors.

Her first tentative steps led her to two Avilese gentlemen – a layman, Francis de Salcedo and a priest, Gaspar Daza. Both were of a rather rigid piety, serious and devout; neither really understood this woman and her mystical flights. Daza, taking it upon himself to 'test' her, treated Teresa far too harshly. She was vulnerable and emotional in the extreme as she adjusted to a life of profound prayer which affected her body and spirit at all levels. She needed gentleness and encouragement whereas she now met with unbending strictness. "He began with the holy determination to treat me as if I were strong" she records, adding that "the distress which it caused me to find that I was not doing as he told me, and felt unable to do so, was sufficient to make me lose hope and give up the whole thing".[2] Salcedo for his part doubted the veracity of her experiences – the devil was at the root of them all! Both asked the advice of other persons in forming their judgements and soon the whole of Avila was buzzing with talk about this nun and her visions. Teresa was mortified at the thought that the townspeople were making her inner life the subject of gossip and public conjecture.

We have to remember that in sixteenth century Spain religion was central. The Inquisition was an established fact, taken for granted by all. It was natural to wonder who was and who was not under suspicion, who was and who was not orthodox, who was or was not a *conversos* and perhaps ready to taint the belief of the Old Christians. Teresa had to be careful lest her ancestry be dragged into the dispute.

Then there were the festivals of the Church which divided up the year and were the cause of holidays for revelling or days of penance. Each village or town had its particular patrons and feasts; hundreds of tapers burned continually at flower-decked shrines and weeping pietas. Dark, sombre churches were frequented by the faithful. There were numerous convents, monasteries and beatorios, each with its designated number of inmates persuing the paths of perfection, mediocrity or even vice. The Catholicism of the day fed upon signs and wonders; and now Avila had its own visionary. The Incarnation, hub of Avilese social life now became the centre of a storm of controversy. One of the nuns was acting in 'singular' fashion. Was it an honour for the city or a disgrace? Teresa in her loneliness and bewilderment was later to lament in her writings:

Oh, what terrible harm is wrought in religious (I am referring now as much to men as to women) when the religious life is not properly observed; when of the two paths that can be followed.... one leading to virtue and the observance of the Rule and the other leading away from the Rule both are frequented almost equally! No, I am wrong: they are not frequented equally for our sins cause the more imperfect road to be the more commonly taken... The way of true religion is frequented so little that, if the friar and the nun are to begin to follow their vocation truly, they need to be more afraid of the religious in their own house than of all the devils.[3]

Teresa sensed the suspicion that surrounded her in her own convent where once she had been a sought-out celebrity. Her self esteem was shaken. Perhaps she *was* possessed by the devil after all!

Eventually Daza and Salcedo advised her to send for a Jesuit. It was the beginning of Teresa's emancipation. This newly founded Society had recently opened a house in town, the College of St Gil, and Fr Juan de Padranos came to hear her confession amidst further public speculation. What could Doña Teresa de Ahumada want with such a learned man? Were not the Carmelite friars sufficient when it came to directing nuns of their own Order? But Fr Padranos proved a good choice. He seemed to understand her perfectly and Teresa's method of prayer was to owe much to Jesuit influence. Padranos "left my soul so tractable it seemed to me there was nothing I feared to undertake".[4] Harshness had paralysed her; gentleness set her free. Under Padranos' direction she progressed along the ascetic path, determined to make up for lost time and not be content to prove her love of God "by words alone". Action was what counted, for "Progress has nothing to do with enjoying the greatest number of consolations in prayer, or with raptures, visions or favours".[5] Rather:

Let there be nothing we know of which it would be a service to the Lord for us to do, and which, with his help, we would not venture to take in hand... We must have a holy boldness, for God helps the strong, being no respecter of persons; and he will give courage to you and me.[6]

An experienced confessor, Padranos knew how to wait on God's hour and he did not try and force Teresa to premature detachments. This had been Daza's weakness – driving rather than leading; a weakness Teresa was to attribute to beginners in the spiritual life, for those who are true proficients have hearts of compassion. In the tradition of the Good Shepherd, Padranos and his successor Fr Baltazar Alvarez allowed Teresa to continue her friendships and receive visitors but advised her to pray sincerely for God to show her his will regarding them. Alvarez would not set rules for his penitent; he trusted that when the time was right God would give her the necessary grace to act accordingly. Pray Teresa did, and in a state of rapture seemed to hear Christ addressing her with the words "I no longer wish you to converse with men but with angels".[7] From that time onwards her friendships were God-directed and she was enabled to break with those people who would have ensnared her in a mediocre existence. Friendships certainly continued (Teresa was sociable and valued close relationships all her life) but they were no longer based on self-satisfaction or vanity and first things came first, for "when conscience enters into anything, friendship does not weigh with me, for I owe more to God than to anyone".[8]

At this point, although progressing steadily, Teresa was as yet unsure of herself. She depended heavily on her confessor and other advisors, her mainstay being Fr Alvarez who continued to guide her. He had scant sympathy with her visions but remained loyal in dark moments when humanly she felt abandoned by others. Near despair she paid a visit to a friend Dona Guioma de Ulloa who lived near the Jesuit church. Here she prayed for several hours and was comforted to hear the Lord speak to her interiorly "Have no fear, it is I. I will not desert you". These words encouraged her for she was still far from being established in inner peace. It was a painful and slow growth, not one accomplished by a miracle dispensing her from effort and pain.

However, her life was beginning to burgeon in holiness, steadfastness in prayer, love for others. People came to recognise these fruits of the Spirit operative in her changed demeanour and enemies gradually became friends and admirers. The Christ whom Teresa loved was forming her into his likeness and the transformation could not be hidden.

Meanwhile Teresa remained at the Incarnation praying, reading, seeking and giving counsel. She was in ripe middle-age, still beautiful but inclined to stoutness. In her brown and cream habit she was the personification of a respected and established religious, matronly and serene, acknowledged to be seriously living her vocation. Yet she was somewhat restless. She felt she should be doing more for God but what should the "something more" consist of? Often with friends she would talk over the early days of the Carmelites, those forebears who were hermits in Palestine and kept the Rule without mitigation; constant in prayer, living in poverty, abstinence and strict reclusion. Ensconced in her own comfortable apartment, surrounded by relatives and sympathetic colleagues, it was pleasant to discourse on Carmel's origins, though it was all in the realm of fantasy as far as Teresa was concerned. She was a professed nun at the Incarnation with its mitigated Rule and "I was most happy in the house where I was, for I was very fond both of the house and of my cell'.[9] Individually she led a more austere life than the rest, but she looked forward to growing old in familiar surroundings. Her heart appreciated the peace and tranquillity of the much loved environment of her youth and conversion. Little did she know she was on the verge of a "second journey". She would be asked to abandon security and set out to become *La Madre*, the foundress.

One evening as she, her two nieces and some other companions talked together about the Church, the way of prayer, the new Orders being founded and the old ones being reformed, one young niece Maria chimed in with the suggestion "Why not become discalced nuns ourselves?"

'Discalced' was a term much used by reforming parties of friars and signified going barefoot rather than shod; it was considered to be symbolic of radical poverty and the spurning of ease.) Teresa was taken aback. She had not thought of herself in the role of reformer – she had had enough to do reforming herself! Then there was the drawback of her age and lack of revenue. Where and how could she start such a venture? She hesitated.

Almost immediately her widowed friend Dona Guiomar came forward to offer money and moral support; the young people she knew were fired with enthusiasm. Teresa could do nothing but bow before the providence of circumstances.

She had an inkling of the labour and suffering that would lie ahead and recoiled on the natural level, but Christ appeared to strengthen her and she rallied. At forty-five she embarked upon her real life-work which would soon take her far from the 'stones and saints' of Avila, see her travel the roads of Spain to open numerous convents, and at last end her life worn out from her exertions, dying of cancer of the womb in a Carmelite cell at Alba de Tormes.

As for the teenager who had so gaily suggested the project: she was to become the grave and self-assured prioress of Valladolid beside whose deathbed would stand the king and queen of Spain seeking a last blessing for themselves and their kingdom.

Teresa was about to set Spain and the world on fire!

NOTES

1. *Way of Perfection*, ch. 7.
2. *Life*, ch. 23.
3. *Life*, ch. 7.
4. *Life*, ch. 24.
5. *Way of Perfection*, ch. 18.
6. *Way of Perfection*, ch. 16.
7. *Life*, ch. 24.
8. *Letter*, 121.
9. *Life*, ch. 32.

Woman of destiny

The foundation of St Joseph's. 1558-62

With her new project in view Teresa began to develop facets of her personality that had so far lain dormant. She had already shown herself to be a woman of the Spirit, immersed in God; the years that followed revealed she had grasped the adage of the monks of old-*age quod agis* – do what you are doing. She proved able to turn her mind from God to the business in hand and be present fully to each as circumstances dictated, for a true contemplative lives in the present with all its ambiguities and not in some far-away realm of 'perfection'. A woman of prayer, she became preeminently a woman of action. Her letters reveal a person of keen insight and business acumen, practical and prosaic as a Castilian housewife.

Above all, Teresa was a 'woman's woman', despite the denigrating remarks on her sex scattered throughout her writings. These were the clichés churchmen expected to hear from a nun vowed to submission yet in every respect as powerful and dominant a figure as themselves. "We women are not so easy to know as you think"[1] she wrote to a priest, and she defended her right to comment on the Song of Songs as a person versed in love rather than in masculine 'learning'.[2] Be that as it may, her genius was certainly expressed in the life she designed for her sisters. This so fitted a woman's psychology by combining wide vistas with attention to detail that the Discalced Carmelites rapidly became the most numerous of contemplative nuns, whereas the male branch of the Order, which she also reformed, never flourished in the same way. Teresa had an intuitive grasp of what was suitable and helpful to those of her sex and enshrined it in practical legislation as well as spiritual insight. A drawback of course, only now coming to the fore, is that women and their role have changed since sixteenth century Spain – her nuns today have to envisage her coping with today's world and women if they are to interpret her spirit aright.

Once Teresa had decided on a foundation of the primitive Rule she set herself to work out the details. It would be a small convent limited to thirteen inmates;[3] strict enclosure would be kept, prayer would form the pivot of the day, the sisters were to work for a living and celebrate a simple liturgy in contrast to the ornate Offices of the larger communities; there was to be poverty and a common life lived in friendship with Christ and with each other. It all seemed an impossible dream! Teresa had no house, no adequate funds, no intending subjects as yet, no official permission to proceed, but she energetically set about preparations, sure that God was behind her. "Not that I am good for anything but I believe God helps those who set out to do great things for his sake and never fails those who trust in him alone"[4] she wrote to her confessor just before the foundation was completed. Teresa was not afraid of 'great things', rather was she distressed by timid folk who appear to be making half-hearted attempts to do things which so far as human reason can judge they can do perfectly well![5]

When Teresa first put her scheme for a convent to her confessor he refused to sanction it but left her free to consult the Carmelite Provincial, Fr Angel de Salazar. She stalled, and craftily sought the advice of men renowned for sanctity, confident that if she could win their backing she would have a better chance of pleading her cause. She forthwith received commendations from St Louis Beltran and St Peter of Alcantara. The latter, a discalced Franciscan of incredible penance and zeal, his body so emaciated that it looked "as if he were made of tree roots" took up her cause as his own and did all he could to further the Reform. He thought women were eminently fitted for totally dedicated lives of prayer and in his opinion the mode of life

Teresa intended to inaugurate would do nothing but good. "He would say that women made much more progress on this road than men, and gave excellent reasons for this, which there is no point in my repeating here, all in favour of women",[6] remarked Teresa gleefully.

With such influential well-wishers, Fr Angel gave Teresa the necessary permission to proceed and Doña Guiomar went looking for a suitable house. But once the town got wind of it uproar ensued. The city did not need another convent! Who was Doña Teresa de Ahumada anyway to think that she could establish some new-fangled way of life? How would the nuns live? Who would provide for their upkeep? All these visions had turned her head. She and her friends were crazy!

Alarmed, Fr Angel backed down, he did not relish facing public disapproval. As for Teresa's sisters at the Incarnation who had viewed the proposed convent as a tacit criticism of their own way of life, they vented their feelings by delighting in her discomforture.

But Teresa was not so easily dissuaded from continuing the fight. She found a champion in the powerful Dominican Fr Pedro Ibanez, who now advanced and won the wavering to Teresa's phalanx, including the recently appointed Jesuit rector Fr Gaspar Salazar. Confidently she returned to the fray, slyly arranging for her sister Juana to purchase a house as if for an Avilan residence for herself and her husband. Teresa engaged workmen and went back and forth discussing alterations to the building, trying to augment Doña Guiomar's slender resources and grateful for a gift of money from her brother Lorenzo in the Indies when she "had not a farthing".[7] His donation arrived just in time to vindicate her trust in Providence.

...but now his Majesty comes and moves you to provide the money; and what amazed me most was that you added those forty pesos, of which I had the greatest need. I think St Joseph, whose name the house is to bear, was not going to let me want for them: I know he will repay you. Poor and small though the house is, it has lovely views and grounds. So that settles the matter of money.[8]

Years later, when Lorenzo returned from the Indies, Teresa took his little daughter into one of her convents and made her an 'honorary Carmelite' until she was old enough to receive the habit as a novice.

It was at Christmas, just as Teresa was bringing her plans to completion and felt her presence to be indispensable for speed and secrecy, that she received a command from the Carmelite Provincial to start at once for Toledo. There Doña Luisa de la Cerda had been plunged into such melancholy at the recent death of her husband that friends despaired of her sanity and even of her life.

Teresa demurred but had no alternative except to obey; she was not an enclosed nun and the Provincial had every right to send her wherever he wished. In January, after a long and cold journey, she and another nun, in company with Juan de Ovalle, her brother-in-law, arrived in Moorish Toledo, the city of her forebears. It was a mysterious city of dark, winding streets, its cathedral and hospital dominating the skyline. Beneath raged the boiling waters of the Tagus swelled by snow, and set back from the road lay the massive palace of Doña Luisa de la Cerda, sorrowing widow of the late Arias Pardo, one of the most powerful grandees of all Spain.

Doña Luisa had asked for Teresa the 'visionary' by name. The nun entered into Spanish high society as naturally as if born to it, making herself at home in the sombre semi-monastic 'court' with its stiff etiquette, sycophants and attendants waiting upon their mistress in strict order of precedence. The experience was salutary:

...I learned how little regard ought to be paid to rank, and how, the higher the rank, the greater are the cares and trials that it brings with it. And I learned that people of rank have to behave according to their state, which

59

hardly allows them to live… often the very food which they eat has more to do with their position than their liking. So it was that I came to hate the very desire to be a great lady. God deliver me from this sinful fuss.[9]

To Teresa it was ridiculous to insist on titles and 'honour' when we all share a common humanity. At Toledo she discerned the grief of the duchess who was after all a woman like herself, with a heart equally vulnerable beneath the trappings of splendour. She had grown spiritually in such a way that she accepted all people as equals and was shocked by nothing. "Let us look at our own shortcomings and leave other people's alone" she was to advise, "for those who live carefully ordered lives are apt to be shocked at everything and we might well learn very important lessons from the persons who shock us'.[10] Teresa, just by being her usual accepting, unshockable self, was a blessing on the whole place. One of her greatest prioresses, Maria de San José, she met here as a young waiting woman. She was to join the reform and govern the Carmel of Seville, though at this stage she was seventeen year old Maria de Salazar, lady-in-waiting to Doña Luisa.

At Toledo too, away from the storm at Avila, Teresa's future plans took new shape when she was visited by an elderly *beata*, Maria de Jesus, who had plans to begin a reformed Carmelite house herself and had actually walked to Rome to obtain the necessary documents. She pointed out that the Primitive Rule of St. Albert decreed that the hermits live without a fixed revenue. Teresa was impressed and decided henceforth not to seek endowments for her own foundation. She conceived a great love for poverty which she nurtured on every level:

Poverty is good and contains within it all good things in the world. It is a great domain. I mean that one who cares nothing for the good things of the world has dominion over them all. What do kings and lords matter to me if I have no desire to possess their money or to please them, if by so doing I should cause the slightest displeasure to God? And what do their honours mean to me if I have realized that the chief honour of a poor person consists in being truly poor.[11]

Later experience led Teresa to modify her view on endowments (it did not sufficiently take into account a woman's inability to be self-supporting in those days) but at this point she fought hard to have the ideal accepted. In this she was fully supported by that Franciscan zealot of poverty, Peter of Alcantara.

Her body in Toledo, her mind in Avila, the Provincial raised his mandate of obedience in June. Teresa could choose whether to stay with Doña Luisa on return to her convent. Teresa opted for the former. The elections were due at the Incarnation and she was afraid lest she be voted in as prioress, something she obviously wished to avoid. But an interior voice reproached her for cowardice, God and the cross awaited her in Avila. She bade Doña Luisa farewell and returned to her city of origin.

As she alighted at the Incarnation she learned that the papal bull authorising her foundation had been received by Doña Guiomar that very day. A group of supporters were gathered to press her cause; chief among these were her confessor Ibanez, and Peter of Alcantara, almost dying, yet unable to depart before he had seen his protegée accepted and established in her Reform. The Bishop, at first dubious, was completely won over by Teresa's charm, and pronounced himself willing to be patron of the foundation rather than letting it fall under the jurisdiction of the Carmelite fathers.

Another happy coincidence was the sickness of her brother-in-law. En route to his house at Alba he contracted a fever and had to rest at the converted 'convent' purchased in his name. Teresa went to nurse him and thus was able, without exciting suspicion, to superintend the final touches to the little "dovecote of the Virgin" whose few inmates were to follow the original Rule of Carmel. Limited numbers would mean selective vocations: Teresa had had enough of large convents filled with uncommitted women.

At last all was ready – the statues of Our Lady and St Joseph set up over the doors and a small cracked bell hung in the belfry. It was on the feast of St Bartholomew, August 24th 1562, that Teresa and a few close friends watched Master Daza give the habit of the Reform to four young women who knelt before the altar in the tiny chapel. Teresa saw them being clothed in the coarse serge habits, the toques of unbleached linen, the white mantles, their feet shod not in shoes and stockings but in the Spanish *alpargatas* of woven rope, designed to move silently along corridors protected from outside interference by thick wooden gratings. The silence of the desert was to be found in the heart of the city within the strict enclosure of St Joseph's.

Today, Teresa's nuns throughout the world commemorate this day as being particularly 'theirs'. The *Te Deum* is sung in Choir as they are united across the years by the same habit, the same ideals, the same poverty and the same love for the Mother who began it all. Teresa's first foundation had been established despite the sneers of the disbelieving. She had seen her dream materialise. God was on her side she was sure. Whatever might befall could not count against this deep conviction in her heart: it was *his* work – he would look after it – and her!

NOTES

1. *Letter*, 121.
2. *Conceptions*, ch. 1.
3. Later legislation placed the limit at twenty-one.
4. *Spiritual Relations*, I.
5. Ibid.
6. *Life*, ch. 40.
7. *Life*, ch. 33.
8. *Letter*, 2.
9. *Life*, ch. 34.
10. *Interior Castle*, Mansion 3, ch. 2.
11. *Way of Perfection*, ch. 2.

Riding out the storm

The early days of the Reform. 1562-63

It is strange how a shining, hopeful song of joy can so quickly turn into a lament of gloom and foreboding. Scarcely a few hours after the ceremony at St Joseph's Teresa found herself plagued by doubts of the severest kind. Had she been disobedient in going ahead without the Provincial's explicit permission? Was it right to have placed her convent under the jurisdiction of the Bishop rather than the Order? Would she herself ever be able to embrace the kind of life practised there? The Incarnation's spacious surroundings contrasted favourably with the confining enclosure of this other house.

Unable even to pray Teresa knelt mutely before the Blessed Sacrament and without any feeling of sensible consolation renewed her commitment. Come what may she would hold firm to her ambition to be a Discalced nun. As she reflected thus her doubts disappeared as speedily as they had materialised:

> ...The devil fled, leaving me quiet and happy; and I have remained so and have been so ever since. All the rules we observe in this house concerning enclosure, penance and other things I find extremely easy and there are not many of them. So great is my happiness that I sometimes wonder what earthly choice I could possibly have made which would be more delightful.[1]

When it came to religious life, Teresa was a 'natural'. She includes her sojourn at the Incarnation when she admits: "I have never known what it is to be discontented with being a nun – not for a single moment of the twenty-eight years and more that have gone by since I became one".[2] This one fleeting moment when she hesitated at St Joseph's was her sole experience of temptation against her vocation and helped her to understand what most people go through as a matter of course. It explains her insistence on the importance of resolution and never giving up once we have embarked on the way of prayer:

...A resolute person fights more courageously. He knows that, come what may, he must not retreat... We must also be firmly convinced from the start that, if we fight courageously and do not allow ourselves to be beaten, we shall get what we want... It is a great thing to have experienced what friendship and joy (the Lord) gives to those who walk on this road.[3]

Meanwhile there was trouble stirring in the town. The citizens of Avila gathered in council to protest against the new convent which had been inaugurated barely before they had got wind of the fact and which had not received the formal permission of the municipality. If the nuns were to live on alms it would take the bread from their children's mouths! Teresa, wanting to vindicate her actions and fearing violence, was just sharpening her wits prior to meeting her opponents when a message arrived from the Incarnation – Doña Teresa's presence was required by the prioress.

It was but two days after the opening of St Joseph's; the town was in an uproar. Teresa obviously wanted to stay with her four novices, yet she was officially a member of the Incarnation, obliged to obey her superior. Still, she had not lost her sense of humour. She returned to her *alma mater* laughing inwardly. She had accomplished what she had wanted, anything else was negligible, and she thought her punishment would be a spell in the convent prison. This would be a welcome break, giving her the opportunity "to rest a little and be alone... all this intercourse with people had worn me to pieces".[4] She felt the need for some solitude and quiet after all the excitement.

But prison was not awaiting her. All that transpired was that she was ordered to account for her actions to the prioress, the community and the Provincial. Teresa did so, explaining herself modestly and humbly, simulating more contrition than she felt. Those who listened found their anger subsiding before her eloquence. In private she spoke more explicitly, convincing the Provincial of her mission and her love for the Order. While Fr Angel did not actually sanction what she had done he declined to put further obstacles in her way. Nevertheless, she had to remain where she was while around St Joseph's the storm seethed on. There was an attempt to batter down the doors and remove the nuns by force. When this failed imprisonment, trial and the disbanding of the group were threatened.

It is hard for us to grasp how such a seemingly trivial matter could arouse the passions of a whole town, but in those days, with each city almost an autonomous state and each person in it closely bound to the others, the business of one was the business of all. It is true too that Spain's whole economy was being undermined by the proliferation of religious houses dependant on alms. The townspeople had a point and they were determined to make it emphatically.

Teresa on the other hand was not devoid of supporters. Those who loved her and valued her work and her person defended her energetically. Daza and Salcedo, by now fully won over to her cause, left no avenue unexplored as they strove to change the course of public opinion. Julian de Avila, brother of one of the novices, a devoted and guileless priest who, as chaplain of St Joseph's was to accompany Teresa on her many journeys, did all he could for the community. What was more, as the town council convened for a learned debate help came from an unexpected quarter. A young Dominican, Fr Domingo Bañez, rose and defended the Reform with eloquence; all the more surprising since he had not as yet met Teresa and was acquainted with her only from hearsay. With the passing years he was to become not only her confessor but one of her most devoted advocates and friends.

"How is this Señores?" (he asked the city fathers satirically) "What the object of this gathering? What foreign enemies threaten these walls? What fire rages through the city? What pestilence consumes it? What famine aflicts it? What ruin is imminent? How can it be that four barefooted nuns – poor, peaceful, virtuous are the cause of so much commotion in Avila? Give me leave to say that to convoke so solemn a meeting for so slight a cause seems to me a lessening of the authority of so grave a city".[5]

When Teresa later gave him the manuscript of the book of her *Life* he found the chapter where she recorded the defense by "a Presentado of the Order of St Dominic"[6] and wrote proudly in the margin: "This happened in the year of 1562, and it was I who gave this counsel, friar Domingo Bañes".

The civic assembly was silenced temporarily by this powerful oratory but soon returned to the attack. Each time the convent was allowed to continue on a temporary basis while a final decision was pending. Fortunately the Bishop was wholly behind Teresa and, as his authority carried great weight, no one wished to oppose him openly. Master Julian went steadily between the Incarnation and the town keeping Teresa abreast of current developments and not minding if he made a bit of a fool of himself. Another priest-supporter, Aranda, actually defended her in Madrid when the council tried to obtain a decree of suppression from the capital.

The weeks dragged on, each side hoping to wear the other down until, more for lack of money to maintain their suit than for any other reason, the city finally desisted. Teresa, a woman without personal financial resources, who had but the richness of her personality and the force of her convictions, won the day, taking in her train the cream of Catholic Avila, now solidly behind her.

Only one query remained. Should she compromise and allow St Joseph's to receive a fixed endowment at least for a time? This would allay any misgivings about the convent being a burden on the city and would show her willingness to meet opponents half-way. Almost convinced of the wisdom behind her reasoning, Teresa was on the verge of signing an agreement to that effect when her ideals reasserted themselves. Had she not vowed poverty? Was her trust in God's providence so lacking? That very night the recently deceased Peter of Alcantara appeared to her in a dream manifesting deep displeasure at what she was about to do. She entertained no further doubts. *Never* would St Joseph's accept a fixed endowment. It was an act of faith in God and a way of distancing herself from the endless quarrels that could ensue when benefactors had to be placated, thinking that because they had offered financial aid they should have a say in how a convent was managed:

> ...For my own part, I believe that honour and money nearly always go together... Understand this clearly, for I think this concern about honour always implies some *slight* regard for endowments or money: seldom or never is a poor person honoured by the world... With true poverty there goes a different kind of honour to which nobody can take objection. I mean, that if poverty is embraced for God's sake alone, no one has to be pleased save God.[7]

Teresa ends her spiritual eulogy on poverty with a practical remark showing her love of independence: "It is certain that a person who has no need of anyone has many friends. I have found this to be very true".[8]

Salcedo registered unfeigned delight at Teresa's decision, as did Fr Bañez, although he had had initial doubts. The townsfolk realised that grumbling and discontent would get them nowhere, and anyway, by this time it was obvious to all that the four novices were leading lives of dedication and prayer. They had remained calm throughout the trouble and in fact so many citizens had begun to take their part that they never lacked food or alms.

Spring came round and all seemed peaceful. Teresa thus persuaded the Carmelite Provincial to allow her to transfer to St Joseph's. She set out with a few poor belongings – a discipline, a straw mat and a hair shirt – accompanied by three nuns from the Incarnation who were to train the novices in religious life and assist them in celebrating the Offices. Tradition has it that, on entering the Church of San Vincente en route to her foundation, Teresa descended to the crypt and there, removing her shoes, symbolically donned the *alpargatas* of a Discalced nun. Then she looked back past the city walls to where the Incarnation stood against the skyline, golden-stoned and warm in the sunshine. She was leaving the cradle of her consecration. At forty-eight Doña Teresa de Ahumada was no more, Madre Teresa of Jesus, the sinner, superseded her.

Trembling with suppressed joy Teresa passed through the door of her new home and knelt in prayer before entering the enclosure. There in the chapel "I all but went into a rapture, and saw Christ who seemed to be receiving me with great love, placing a crown on my head and thanking me for all I had done for his mother."[9]

So began for Teresa the few years of seclusion she was ever to know. They were certainly not years of inactivity even though for a time she passed from the public eye. She revised and rewrote the story of her *Life* (which she had begun while at Dona Luisa's house in Toledo) and composed the *Way of Perfection* for her nuns in which she outlined her own conception of the Carmelite vocation if it was to be truly a life of prayer. During these years she lived fully the Rule she had vowed to reinstate in its primitive rigour, but lived it in such a way that all seemed sweet because all was in the service of Christ her supreme Love. The legacy she was destined to leave to posterity was attested by no less a churchman than her famous contemporary Luis de Leon who, as editor of her *Works*, prefaced them with a letter addressed to the prioress of the Madrid Carmel.

I never knew or saw Mother Teresa of Jesus while she lived on earth; but now that she lives in heaven I do know her, and I see her almost continuously in two living images of herself which she left us – her daughters and her books... If I were to see her features, they would reveal her physical self, and if I were to hear her words, they would tell me something concerning the virtue of her soul. But the first of these things would be very commonplace and the second might be deceptive, whereas neither of these disadvantages attaches to the two ways in which I see her now... It is the fruits which each of us leaves when he dies that are the true witness to his life.[10]

NOTES

1. *Life*, ch. 36.
2. Ibid.
3. *Way of Perfection*, ch. 23.
4. *Life*, ch. 36.
5. From a contemporary source quoted in *Santa Teresa, Her Life and Times*, by G. Cunninghame Graham, p. 237.
6. *Life*, ch. 36.
7. *Way of Perfection*, ch. 2.
8. Ibid.
9. *Life*, ch. 36.
10. *Letter*, from master Fray Luis de Léon. Found in the *Appendix* to the *Complete Works*.

A garden enclosed

Teresa's Rule of Life in spirit and practice

"People say this is a new Order and accuse us of inventing new things. Let them read our Primitive Rule, for what we follow is simply that Rule without mitigation, with the rigour originally prescribed by the Pope".[1] So wrote Teresa who was intensely conscious of her full Carmelite heritage (though she was unaware that technically speaking she was following the Rule as sanctioned by Innocent IV in 1247, different in some minor respects from that written by St Albert). Her one idea was to restore to Carmel its tradition of prayer and solitude in the manner of the first hermits who had gathered on the holy mountain for this purpose and whose Rule revolved around the kernel sentence: "Each of you is to stay in his own cell or nearby pondering on the Lord's law day and night and keeping watch at his prayers unless attending to some other duty".[2]

However, it would be a fallacy to suppose that Teresa merely resurrected a form of life that had once been followed and then forsaken. Times change and what suits one period of history does not necessarily suit another. The Innocentian Rule envisioned quite literally a community of hermits, each one dwelling in a separate hermitage and gathering only for daily Mass, common meals and the Office. While being a reformer Teresa was no religious antiquarian. She was a creative innovator; a foundress who based her legislation on St Albert's ideals, looking to the first hermits for inspiration but not slavishly following their exterior expression of the charism. Her return to sources was no exaltation of a historical past for its own sake. The heart of a hermit was her aim:

All of us who wear the sacred habit of Carmel are called to prayer and contemplation – because we are descended from the line of those holy fathers of ours of Mount Carmel who sought this treasure, this precious pearl of which we speak, in such solitude and with such contempt of the world.[3]

Teresa envisaged a small group of nuns, earning their daily bread as far as possible, each one wanting a closer union with Christ in prayer. They would support one another in the quest for God, living in a family-type community but fostering a wholly eremitical spirit.

Teresa had suffered from the custom of being allowed out of her convent for visits and social occasions so she regulated for a very strict enclosure to approximate the desert. Within the enclosure there had to be all that was necessary for a full Christian and religious life: sufficient intellectual stimulation, human companionship, grounds for exercise, a few hermitages to which the sisters could withdraw from time to time for periods of uninterrupted prayer. Spiritual nourishment was meagre in that there was a lack of good literature available for women; nuns were not expected to read Latin and religious books in the vernacular were hard to come by. Translations of the Bible were forbidden though Teresa treasured up all the quotations that she could glean from the liturgy or sermons. Hence her insistence on learned men being appointed to give direction and hear her nuns' confessions. In her estimation a learned man was better than a pious but uneducated priest whose views lacked balance and discretion, for "learning is a great help in giving light upon everything".[4] Prayer must be founded upon the rock of a properly formed conscience, and her sisters needed liberty to consult whomsoever they wished. Quite an innovation – they were expected to have minds of their own!

It might be presumed by the uninitiated that Teresa's emphasis on prayer, strict enclosure, mortification, would create an oppressive or gloomy atmosphere, but this was far from being the case. There was a lightness and joy in her convents, a concern with practicalities and persons that bore the stamp of the foundress's own gladsome spirit.

The nuns of St Joseph's were expected, not to be wrapped up each in her own concerns, but open to all the others in the community – offering love, support, companionship, even fun, for Teresa insisted on a twice daily recreation to which all were to come:

> Try sisters to be as pleasant as you can, without offending God, and to get on as well as you can with those you have to deal with, so that they may like talking to you... and not be frightened and put off by virtue. This is very important for nuns: the holier they are the more sociable they should be with their sisters.[5]

Teresa herself was a talented entertainer, and with outside amusements barred she and the sisters knew how to make their own. We hear of her dancing with castanets, leading processions, writing amusing verses, celebrating Clothing and Profession ceremonies with poems and songs of her own devising; a rotund, dark and flashing Spaniard goading her nuns playfully on:

> Like Elias we must go,
> All his zeal and courage show,
> Conquering nature here below,
> *Nuns of Carmel*[6]

Once we are told she went into ecstasy at an Eastertide recreation when a novice with a beautiful voice sang with exquisite purity;

> Let my eyes see thee, sweetest Jesu, nigh,
> Let me eyes see thee, then I shall die.[7]

Teresa admitted a few very young girls to her houses and delighted in their innocent games. Everything about her was fully human and she wanted her sisters to be so too. When one nun absented herself from recreation "to pray" Teresa was indignant at such behaviour and called her a "sour face". Her niece testified that "Outwardly, indeed, she was so natural and so courteous that no one who looked at her would think there was anything of the saint about her at all."[8]

In her appreciation of the need for growth in the social virtues Teresa emphasised community as much as solitude. The experience of solitude is only fruitful if there is an atmosphere of deep love. Community living fosters this through friendship: "Here all must love one another, help one another, care for one another".[9] It is also a check on the natural self-centredness that can easily predominate unless a person is well purified. As Teresa indicates – it is all very well to think we are virtuous when we are alone, but living with others and coping with 'rubs' proves whether or not we actually are.

> If a person is always recollected, however holy he may think himself to be, he does not know if he is patient and humble and has no means of knowing it. A man may be very strong, but how can he be sure if he has not proved himself in battle?... I think it is a greater favour if the Lord sends us a single day of humble self-knowledge, even at the cost of many afflictions and trials, than many days of prayer... It would be a bad business if we could practice prayer only by getting alone in corners.[10]

If it is in community living that virtue is tested, it is in solitude that we can explore the depths of our hearts with all their hidden weaknesses. Prayer that has no element in it of aloneness, of solitude before the Lord, can never go deep. This takes time to develop. It needs patience with self and with others and it demands a long discipline in the school of love, a discipline firm yet mild, for "we must proceed diligently and lovingly rather than severely".[11]

73

Teresa warned against being too impatient with self and others, judging them unkindly, foisting upon them one's own rigid or impossibly high standards, spreading an atmosphere of gloom. "In the early stages (of the spiritual life) we should strive to be happy and free" she wrote, for "discretion is necessary throughout".[12] We have to be understanding of ourselves as human beings with needs, feelings, desires. Accepting our human condition is to build on the sure foundation of truth and humility: "To be humble is to walk in truth".[13]

The *Way of Perfection*, ostensibly written to teach the nuns of St Joseph's about prayer, is in fact a treatise on the ascetical rather than the mystical life. It is rightly a classic of spiritual literature applicable to all. Martha and Mary are both needed, both have a contribution to make. "Remember that there must be someone to cook the meals and count yourselves happy to be able to serve like Martha.... What should it matter to us if we do one thing rather than another?"[14] Prayer is not about 'saying prayers' but about living the Gospel with all the implications involved for daily behaviour:

Consider, daughters, that whether we wish it or no, God's will must be done both in heaven and on earth. Believe me, then, do as I suggest and make a virtue of necessity.

Teresa sets her teaching on prayer in the context of a life involving three elements: love of others, detachment, humility. Without these there can be no progress. She deals separately with each in turn, laying special stress on humility. This is a topic to which she returns continually; it is, she says, the most necessary of all virtues and she never changes her mind on this point.

In her most mature work, the *Interior Castle*, she reiterates the theme of humility with renewed insistence. Using the image of the soul as a castle, Teresa depicts the way to the centre where the King dwells as being a journey passing through a series of *Mansions* or dwelling places. She does not pretend that she can enumerate them all, rather she contents herself with describing seven, which take the reader from the outskirts of the castle to the most interior rooms, in the last of which the traveller is united to the Lord of the castle, Christ. The route into the fortress is by way of humility. With humility we grow in the knowledge of self and of God (for these are linked). There is no substitute for this, no technique which will enable us to dispense with the early spadework. We cannot even begin to know God without humility; it is the doorway into ourselves, and how can we know God if we are unable to live with the person we are in truth rather than in imagination!

One of the results of genuine humility as Teresa understands it is that it does not leave us downcast; we don't bemoan our state: "All is lost... if only I hadn't... nobody will love me now... I never had a chance..." To be truly humble is to be rooted in the soil of God. He becomes our ground, we find security and peace in darkness and trust, whatever we may or may not have done. Here Teresa is a great example. She knew she had been unfaithful in her own life but she never ceased trusting in God's mercy, nor did she allow others to despair either. If we have sinned (and who has not?) we have only to recognise the fact, humble ourselves, and the earth (*humus*) is prepared for the living, life-giving water which comes with prayer.

As for the question of 'honour' (*honra*) so prevalent in Teresa's milieu, she is absolutely uncompromising. No humility, no detachment, no mutual love can take root where people are concerned with their rights, their privileges, their 'dignity' for these are contrary to all that the Gospel stands for. She knew from experience that "there is no poison so fatal to perfection".[16] She had experienced the shame, the fear of exposure, the lack of security that followed the family of the *conversos* from cradle to grave in a society that set such store by 'pure blood'. In her convents the family name was to be dropped and all talk of ancestry outlawed: "Our only honour, sisters, is to serve the Lord".[17] Also, all respect for rank and privilege was anathema, incompatible with following Christ in poverty and detachment.

> God deliver us from people who try to serve him yet who care for their honour and fear disgrace. What we gain by this only does us harm: as I said honour is lost by those who seek it; above all by religious, especially in the matter of rank... You may think that this is a trifling fault and only human nature; that it is of no importance. Do not hold it lightly; it spreads in monasteries as quickly as foam gathers on water. Nothing can be called trifling in so great a danger as these points of honour and sensitiveness to affronts.[18]

If any sister should be of such a temperament and indulges in this fault Teresa advises the prioress to:

> Drive away this plague; cut off the branches as well as you can; and, if that is not sufficient pull up the roots... Oh, what a great evil this is! God deliver us from a convent where it enters: I would rather our convent caught fire and we were all burned alive.[19]

Here we see *La Madre* at her most powerful, the sister of fighting *conquistadores*, the woman who asked everything from her nuns and who had no patience with any form of compromise.

In the *Way* Teresa was not writing for proficient prayers but for those taking the first steps: for eager young girls who came seeking a life of total self-giving yet knowing not where or how to begin. This book is a proof that Carmel is not for mystical high-flyers but for women whose feet are firmly on the ground, who are prepared to enter into close relationships with others and are not afraid of the pain of self-exposure. Teresa certainly asks everything, but everything given progressively, prayer and life going hand in hand from the very first stages onwards. And she phrases her teaching in a tone of graciousness, understanding and even gentle teasing for:

This house is another heaven, if it be possible to have heaven on earth. Anyone whose sole pleasure lies in pleasing God will find our life a very good one; if she wants anything more she will lose everything, for there is nothing more that she can have.[20]

NOTES

1. *Letter*, 252.
2. *Rule of St Albert*. The complete rule is given in the Appendix of this book.
3. *Interior Castle*, Mansion 5, ch. 1.
4. *Way of Perfection*, ch. 5.
5. *Way of Perfection*, ch. 41.
6. *Poems*, no. 10.
7. *Spiritual Relations*, no. 15. The singer was Isabel de Jesus, a novice in the Carmelite convent at Salamanca.
8. Testimony of Sr Teresa of Jesus (the Saint's neice) in the *Appendix* to the *Complete Works*.
9. *Way of Perfection*, ch. 4.
10. *Foundations*, ch. 5.
11. *Way of Perfection*, ch. 4.
12. *Life*, ch. 13.
13. *Interior Castle*, Mansion 6, ch. 10.
14. *Way of Perfection*, ch. 17.
15. *Way of Perfection*, ch. 32.
16. *Way of Perfection*, ch. 12.
17. *Way of Perfection*, ch.2.
18. *Way of Perfection*, ch. 12.
19. *Way of Perfection*, ch. 7.
20. *Way of Perfection*, ch. 13.

Woman and warrior

The apostolate of holiness and its extension.
1567

For Teresa, prayer was a definite apostolate. She was contemporary with the Council of Trent; the Church was in
drastic need of reform and Luther's doctrine was spreading
and gaining the ascendancy in many countries. Teresa had
a sense of urgency – time was passing and what contribution was *she* making to the current situation "a woman and
a sinner"[1] though she be? She was therefore not interested
in establishing a Benedictine-type "school of the Lord's
service" with its daily round of solemn Offices, extensive
land cultivation, leisure for holy reading and a variety of
crafts and charitable enterprises which could provide a
place for large numbers of people. She was setting up a
"fortress" of "picked soldiers"[2] who would fight to the
death for the Church and her Lord. "We must make some
progress, however little, every day and show some increase
in fervour. We ought to act as if we were at war - as indeed
we are – and never relax until we have won the victory"[3]
she wrote to her brother Lorenzo.

Unlike Benedict who prescribed that prayer should be
short and fervent when the monk was moved by grace,
Teresa legislated for two hours of private mental prayer a day
and a less time-consuming manner of reciting the Office:

> The singing must never be with modulations, but in
> monotone. Usually let everything be said, and this holds
> for Mass too: the Lord will see to it that there is a little
> time over for earning what we need.[4]

In this approach she was obviously influenced by her
close links with the Jesuit and Dominican Orders, both of

which at various times supplied her confessors and were strongly apostolic in outlook. Prayer *was* effective action in Teresa's mind. By means of it her nuns would win graces for those who had to carry Christ into the world – to its palaces, prisons and parishes. By mortification and continual intercession ("prayer and self-indulgence do not go together"[5]) the Carmelite nuns would take the place of Moses on the mountain, who ensured Israel's triumph over its enemies by keeping his hands raised in supplication while the battle raged in the plain beneath. Theirs was to be a life of sustained prayer, sustained passion, for "one moment of pure love is more useful to the Church than all good works put together, though it seem that nothing were done"[6]. A woman of her time had no place in the ecclesiastical world apart from the cloister, thus Teresa took a special interest in those who had to do combat in the arena of theological debate and pastoral ministry. If priests were not holy what kind of example would the ordinary Christian have to follow?

Teresa was certainly happy at St Joseph's. She organised the cooking on a rota basis and took her weekly turn when it came round just like anyone else. She cared for the sick, commissioned repair work trusting in the Lord to provide the workmen's wages for "she hadn't a farthing'.[7] There was joy too in forming her young sisters who all seemed set upon holiness and obedience; but she was growing restless. Even 'holy' pleasures were insufficient when there was much to be accomplished. Love needed to be proved by action, and Teresa was a thorough extrovert.

Already she was becoming as attached to her new little community as she had been to the Incarnation. Her austere cell, the homely kitchen with its brass pans and roaring fire, the chapter room from whose simple prioress's chair (noticeably contrasting in style from an abbess's throne) she had given conferences to her sisters, the garden with its fine view over the countryside, the hermitage with the picture of "the Christ with the beautiful eyes"... all were full of memories for her. Yet this eremitical community life needed to spread elsewhere. More "picked troops" were required. Numbers at St Joseph's were limited and, in any case, women were not expected to travel far to convents; they tended to remain in or near their place of birth. So Teresa set her sights farther afield. She had a mission to accomplish – her whole self was at God's disposal. She could pray sincerely:

Do thou strengthen and prepare my soul first of all, Good of all good, my Jesus, and do thou then ordain means whereby I may do something for thee. For no one could bear to receive as much as I have done and pay nothing in return. Cost what it may, Lord, permit me not to come into thy presence with such empty hands, since a person's reward will be in accordance with his works. Here is my life, here is my honour and my will, I have given it all to thee. I am thine, dispose of me according to thy desire. Well do I know, Lord, of how little I am capable. But now that I have approached thee, now that I have mounted this watchtower whence truths can be seen, I shall be able to do all things provided thou withdraw not from us.[8]

Four years had passed and Teresa was more than ready to be up and doing once more. The spur was given by a Franciscan friar, Alonso Maldonado, just returned from the Indies. He preached on the tragic number of natives being 'lost' for lack of instruction in the Christian religion. Greatly moved, Teresa longed to do something about it. Doubtless, in the manner of the times, Maldonado envisaged all unbaptised South American Indians as destined for hell; and since her own vision of hell Teresa had a strong desire to see that others avoided going to such a place.

Barely six months after Maldonado's inspiring oratory the Carmelite General was in Avila on visitation. Summoned to Spain by Philip II to implement the decrees of the Council of Trent, John Baptist Rossi (Rubeo) was the first head of the Order to come to Castile. His most Catholic

Majesty, who had invited him, wished to see his subjects tread the paths of austerity and virtue.

Rubeo went first to Seville in Andalusia where recalcitrant friars had given grave scandal, especially three blood brothers, Balthasar, Melchoir and Gaspar Nieto. All three were later to renounce the mitigated Rule of the Calced and find refuge with the Discalced friars, bringing to the Teresian Reform greater friction than peace by their continual feuds and insubordination. From Seville, where the General's reforming measures were met with scorn and abuse, Rubeo proceeded to a Chapter of friars at Avila. On hearing of his presence in the city Teresa invited him to St Joseph's and spoke earnestly of her desires and plans for expansion. Instead of being annoyed with her as she had feared (after all, she had left the Incarnation and placed her own foundation under the Bishop rather than the Order) the elderly priest warmed immediately to *La Madre* and her companions. He could scarcely believe she had accomplished so much at a time when the Order in Spain was in a noticeable decline. He forthwith gave her every encouragement to found convents wherever she chose, his only stipulation being that she keep within the boundaries of Castile.

It had occurred to Teresa that she might also extend the reform to men. On this score Rubeo was naturally more hesitant. His reception by the Carmelites of Andalusia had been inauspicious and he had found it impossible to persuade them to adopt a stricter form of religious life or even one with minimal conformity to the vows they had professed. How could a woman succeed where a man of authority had failed? A woman moreover who was bound by enclosure and hampered by prejudice against her sex. He considered the matter, and before departing from Spain at the end of his visitation the General sent her from Barcelona[9] an authorisation to found two Discalced friaries which would be subject to the Spanish Provincial of the Order.

Teresa was jubilant. Everything she desired had been granted by the Order's highest authority. True, at present there was only St Joseph's, but in her mind's eye she pictured the Reform spreading and prospering. Her first venture would be a house at nearby Medina del Campo. From there she would look for friars to begin her other project, though where they would come from mystified her "seeing how few there were in this province – it seemed to me they were dying out".[10] Teresa had plenty of "patents and good wishes"[11] – what she lacked, but felt sure of finding, were people who would carry her plans into effect. Yet twenty years afterwards Fray Luis de Leon could eulogise:

> Spain is now full of her houses, in which God is served by more than a thousand religious... Just as it was one blessed woman who gave birth to this Reform, so it is women who take the lead in it throughout, and not only are they guiding lights to their Order but they are the honour of our nation, the glory of this age... living witnesses to the efficacy of Christ, clear proofs of his sovereign virtue and exact patterns in which we can almost experience what faith promises.[12]

NOTES

1. *Way of Perfection*, ch. 1.
2. *Way of Perfection*, ch. 3.
3. *Letter* 2.
4. *Primitive Constitutions*. The Order's official English translation.
5. *Way of Perfection*, ch. 10.
6. *A Spiritual Canticle*, by John of the Cross. Stanza XXIX. Lewis translation.
7. *Deposition* of Mother Mary of St Jerome, Teresa's cousin, in the *Appendix* of the *Complete Works*.
8. *Life*, ch. 21.
9. Teresa mistakenly wrote 'Valencia' in the *Foundations*. The patent is dated 14 August 1567.
10. *Foundations*, ch. 2.
11. Ibid.
12. Fray Luis de Leon, *op. cit.*

A city taken by storm

The foundation of Medina del Campo.
August 1567

Medina del Campo in the sixteenth century was a cosmo-
politan centre where trade flourished. Its regular fairs
brought merchants together from all over Europe. Ger-
mans, Flemings, Genoese, Frenchmen and Englishmen
rubbed shoulders as they haggled over and handled tapestries, fine cloth, silk, leather and gewgaws of all kinds. "No
office for the King. No benefice for the Pope" was
emblazoned on the arms of a city which prided itself on its
financial stability, orthodox piety and strong spirit of independence. Teresa felt sure she would find women there
who wanted the full rigours of Discalced Carmelite life,
and she already had a prospective novice (for whom there
was no vacancy at St Joseph's) offering her modest dowry
as part-rent for whatever building could be acquired as a
convent.

In Medina Teresa also had influential friends – Fr
Balthazar Alvarez, rector of the Jesuit college and her one
time confessor, and Fr Antonio Heredia, prior of the
Medina Carmelite friary, who had until recently been prior
at Avila. The latter had promised to look for a suitable
place for her nuns and assured them of a welcome from
the populace. In fact the house which he deemed suitable
was so far from being so that Fr Julian in despair went to
find another.

Still, Teresa was full of confidence in everyone's good
will and needed no second invitation. She gathered together a nucleus of sisters for the new community; of these
four were chosen from the Incarnation, (two of them cousins of hers who, despite opposition, decided to throw in
their lot with the Reform). Two she took from St Joseph's,

one of them her niece Maria Bautista, the former Maria de Ocampo who had first posited a Discalced foundation on that memorable day several years ago when she and others sat around Teresa in her cell at the Incarnation. It seemed that Medina was almost a family affair. Relatives could be an asset at times!

As for St Joseph's – the citizens of Avila thought that convent would "go to pieces immediately", if the charismatic prioress departed. They conjectured that its continuance depended on the presence of this woman but, like the true leader she was, Teresa had trained up responsible successors and was able to leave her sisters in the care of a subordinate, though as was only natural "she herself felt the parting very keenly but tried to hide her feelings lest she should distress us".[2]

La Madre decided that August 15th would be a suitable festival on which to inaugurate the new convent; so on the 11th (Medina was two days' journey from Avila) she and her party set off. They travelled in a covered cart, the canvas securely fastened in front to maintain enclosure even while on the road. Inside in the stifling heat the nuns kept their regular hours of prayer and recreation, Teresa ringing a bell to indicate the time. Outside the muleteers cursed and sang by turns, accompanied by the noise of copper cooking utensils and other luggage on a hammock beneath. The young nuns, eager and excited at travelling in unfamiliar terrain squinted out of the cracks in the canvas when Teresa was wrapt in her devotions. No doubt she saw them but turned a blind eye to this infraction of the rules. After all, they had seldom if ever left the confines of Avila in their lives and she was not one to despise an innocent spirit of adventure.

The group left Avila openly, despite jeers and general scepticism about the outcome of the trip. Teresa herself had no misgivings. Had she not an excellent guide in her chaplain, Fr Julian? Had she not friends expecting her arrival? Had not the license been obtained and the city's permission willingly granted? Was not a house awaiting them into which they had only to move and begin their regular life? All was well.

They stopped overnight at Arévalo and there disastrous news was brought from Medina: the Augustinian Friars were raising objections to the house Fr Julian had rented on Teresa's behalf and which the men considered too near their own. The message was that the nuns were not to leave Avila until the business had been sorted out – yet here they were already half way to their destination! To return the way they had come would only excite more mockery than had attended their departure. So much for the expanding Reform!

Teresa's friend, Fr Domingo Bañez, happened to be in Arévalo when the party arrived. He joined Teresa in anxious consultation. She was resolved to keep the impending tragedy secret from her nuns lest they lose heart. Four of them (those from the Incarnation) were forthwith sent to stay with a priest relative; the other two were to proceed to Medina with Teresa and Fr Julian. Fr Antonio, the Carmelite prior, who had also come out to meet them, assured them they could still have the use of the first house he had tried to purchase. It was theirs, even if not very suitable for habitation as yet.

Arriving in Medina at midnight on the eve of the Assumption ("Our Lady in August" as the festival was commonly called) the group knocked up the startled Carmelite friars. Presently, by torchlight the travellers could be seen flitting to and fro, gathering vestments, ornaments and sacred vessels for Mass. When all was ready they sneaked out in procession – priests, friars, nuns, carrying their booty, ready to take possession of the house before the city was aware of what was happening. They had forgotten that on the eve of such a great feast the bulls would be being penned for the night prior to the festal bullfight, but fortunately they did not happen upon any animals.[3] Swiftly and silently they made their way along the deserted streets to their destination, looking like "a party of gypsies" as Fr Julian wryly remarked.

At this late hour Teresa was unprepared for what met her eyes. The proposed convent was even more of a ruin than she had anticipated. Fr Antonio, she said, must be blind if he had ever considered such a place suitable for reserving the Blessed Sacrament! The porch, which he had assured them could be turned into a temporary chapel, was unplastered; there were holes in the roof and the whole building so dilapidated that Teresa felt close to despair. Still, here she was. She had travelled to Medina to spread the Reform, and here she would stay, even if this was the only site available.

Quickly she tucked up her habit and set to work. Doña Teresa de Ahumada, since coming to reside at St Joseph's, had learned to wield bucket and mop. This was to stand her in better stead for the work of her foundations than any number of interior locutions.

She turned her attention next to the porch walls. Perhaps they would not look too disreputable if adorned with some hangings. Those the nuns had brought with them proved insufficient, but an offer of tapestries and a blue damask bedspread were gratefully received. Then they needed nails to hang them with. Teresa scanned the walls for extras of this precious commodity and extracted what she could without bringing more of the building down around her.

The porch thus arrayed in various wallhangings and draped bedding, Teresa and her nuns scrubbed and polished the remainder of the dawn hours away, while a notary was summoned from his sleep to attest the establishment of a new convent. The bell was then duly rung and curious passers-by found themselves witnessing the first Mass being celebrated in the new Monastery of St Joseph. The Discalced nuns had come to Medina del Campo! Teresa had triumphed. Well could she sit back and relax, rubbing her work-worn hands in contentment.

The triumph was exceedingly short lived. In full daylight the house appeared to be in an even worse condition than Teresa had conjectured when the sky was still dusky. The walls were not only shaky but actually falling down in several places (their sturdiness somewhat wanting and doubtless aggravated by the removal of the nails for the hangings). Teresa was afraid to leave the Blessed Sacrament unattended in such an environment where possible heretic merchants might commit sacrilege. She hired watchmen to guard the tabernacle and herself rose during the night to check that they were assiduously engaged in their duty and not dozing.

It was obvious that another house would have to be found but none seemed available. At last, after a week of anxiety, a merchant offered Teresa and her sisters the top floor of his own mansion and there they stayed while their own convent was being adapted and put in order. Later a little chapel was built, thanks to the generosity of the niece of the Grand Inquisitor of Spain who, together with her daughter, became a Discalced nun at the Medina Carmel, adding the glory of the name of Quiroga to the Reform.

While in the city Teresa was not only occupied with her own nuns but with the propagation of her ideals among the friars. She discussed these plans in confidence with Fr Antonio, the prior who had been so imprudent in a choice of convent for them. He was a pious man but lacking in commonsense, rather narrow minded and rigid, wholly wrapped up in affairs of no moment. Imagine Teresa's amazement when he offered to be her first recruit: "I took that as a joke and told him so".[4] She obviously did not think him at all suitable for what she had in mind, although she was too polite to say so bluntly. Instead she suggested he try living according to the primitive Rule in the place where he already was. He was offended at the implications and told her he was in fact considering a transfer to the Carthusians and had already been accepted by them. Surely if such men found him able for their life of austerity a woman need have no scruple on that score. Teresa was unconvinced. Antonio was old and querulous as it was; at his age she envisaged no great improvement and time proved her correct. Still, his good will was not to be scorned. Let him wait awhile and be tested; maybe he would prove a 'companion-friar' if someone else could be found.

At this point another embryonic Carthusian aspirant from the Carmelite Order turned up – a diminutive man of twenty-five, barely five foot in height, burning with fervour and the desire for a more perfect life. Teresa had eventually met her spiritual counterpart in John of St Matthias, the future St John of the Cross (for like Teresa he took a new name when he embraced the Reform). Like her, he too was of *conversos* stock and had joined the Carmelites at the age of twenty-one. His childhood however, unlike hers, had been spent in extreme poverty. John's father, marrying for love, had been disinherited by his family. They considered the bride socially beneath them and were, like all *conversos*, afraid of any stain on their lineage being investigated and bringing disaster on their fragile and dearly won position in Spanish society.[5]

When his father died John was seven or eight years old. His mother Catalina was forced to find work as a weaver to feed her three sons, of whom John was the youngest. The second son died as a result of privation and the family moved to Medina del Campo in a desperate attempt to find employment. John tried his hand at several trades but proved to have scant aptitude for any but nursing. Part of his youth was spent caring for syphilitics in the hospital of *las Bubas*; but his natural piety asserted itself when it came to deciding on a permanent commitment and he entered the Carmelite house of St Anne at Medina in preference to the secular priesthood.

The Order sent John to pursue studies at the University of Salamanca where he was considered a brilliant student. He had a methodical and penetrating mind, a keenness to excel and a horror of compromise. Since his noviciate days he had kept the primitive Rule without mitigation, making himself unpopular among his contemporaries – they found his zeal somewhat unnerving. Time was to soften him until at the end of his life he was known as the gentlest and most compassionate of men.

Teresa recognised in John the one who would initiate the form of life she had in mind for friars, combining contemplation with an active apostolate. She dissuaded him from the Carthusians and promised he could soon be a Discalced Friar – her very first – and she instructed him accordingly. There was never as strong a bond between these two as later historians have tried to imply, nor did Teresa ever take John as her spiritual director; but there was mutual respect of each others holiness and a shared ideal despite wide differences of temperament and up-bringing. Introducing John to a friend of hers Teresa wrote:

I beg you to have a talk with this father and help him in his undertaking for, small of stature though he is, I believe he is great in the sight of God. We shall certainly miss him here sorely for he is a sensible person and well fitted for our way of life, so I believe our Lord has called him to this work... Although we have had some disagreements here over business matters, and I have been the cause of them and have sometimes been vexed with him, we have never seen the least imperfection in him. He has courage; but as he is quite alone he needs all the Lord gives him so that he may do his work well... He is very much given to prayer and most intelligent.[6]

Teresa admired John ("People look upon him as a saint, which, in my opinion, he is and has been all his life"[7]) but never really understood him – perhaps it was more that John himself retained his emotional independence from *La Madre* – there are hints of this even in the above letter written when they were not long acquainted.

But as things stood at present Teresa had at Medina "a friar and a half", the half friar a teasing reference to John's stature as the phrase is usually taken, but it has ambiguous undertones. Maybe Antonio was the "half friar" in her estimation? She had felt a need to test him, whereas John needed no testing, for "though he was living among the

Calced fathers of the Observance, he had always led a life of great perfection and religious zeal".[8] These two men she resolved to use as foundation stones for a Discalced friary, to materialize when conditions were favourable.

Meanwhile she invited John to learn all he could about the life – perhaps joining in the nuns' recreations would dispel some of that 'stiffness' of his. She was a great believer in feminine companionship when it came to bringing people down to earth, "it does good to hear a little entertaining chatter".[9] On completing his studies John travelled with Teresa to Valladolid to experience the Discalced spirit at first hand by constant contact with her sisters. He could then transpose it to the men who would join him in the future.

NOTES

1. Testimony of Mother Mary of St Jerome, *op. cit.*
2. Ibid.
3. Cf *Foundations*, ch. 3.
4. Ibid.
5. John's lineage is treated at some length by R. Harvey in his *Search for Nothing* the life of St John of the Cross.
6. *Letter*, 10.
7. *Letter*, 204.
8. *Foundations*, ch. 13.
9. *Letter*, 126.

The spread of the Reform

Foundations at Malagon, Valladolid, Pastrana, Duruelo, Toledo, Salamanca and Alba de Tormes. 1568-71

The next four years were incredibly busy ones for Teresa. Having started on her foundations it seemed that opportunities were opening everywhere. Between August 15th 1567 and July 10th 1571 when she was asked to return to the Incarnation as prioress, she had founded seven convents of her own: Medina, Malagon, Valladolid, Toledo, Pastrana, Salamanca and Alba de Tormes. She had also reformed one at Alcala. This was the house established by Sr Maria de Jesus, the elderly *beata* whom Teresa had met while staying with Doña Luisa prior to the inauguration of St Joseph's. As self-styled prioress she had introduced at Alcala a regime of harsh austerity where her nuns were vying with each other in the use of penitential instruments of all kinds, from chains to hair shirts. Teresa moved in and did what she could to restore a sense of proportion. She lightened the atmosphere by encouraging periods of recreation and the more gentle and tolerant outlook favoured in her own convents. Then she presented the sisters with her *Constitutions* and returned (thankfully no doubt, for her task at Alcala must have demanded infinite tact) to her role as foundress.

Teresa in these years also established the two houses for friars for which the General had previously given permission. The first at Duruelo, a tiny hamlet, where in a veritable barn John of the Cross, Antonio and two companions began life according to the Primitive Rule. They had to face a life of great poverty in those early days: "The only articles with which (Antonio) was well provided were clocks, of which he had five. I thought that very amusing".[1] His idea was to be sure they kept regular hours even if they had nothing to sleep on! The second friary was at Pastrana, where Teresa received two eccentric Italian hermits into the Order, the decrees of the Council of Trent having stated that all independent religious should join an authorised group. The elder of the hermits, Mariano, was of an explosive and fiery temperament who amused himself with subterranean engineering (in which he had formerly been employed by the king). His companion betrays his character in his religious name – John of the Misery. Pastrana was later to become the centre of much controversy as the type of men incorporated into the Discalced were drawn from such diverse backgrounds, unformed by Teresa who had difficulty in really knowing how they should develop: she never had such a sureness of touch with the male branch of the Order as with her nuns. The novice master appointed to train new recruits took to imposing outlandish penances and had to be removed from office, being replaced by John of the Cross. This was a recurring plaint – youth and zeal are no substitute for maturity and experience, whether in men or women. After a similar failure with a young prioress Teresa wrote:

...In some ways we allowed them too much freedom, and we ought not to have put so much trust – or any trust at all – in people who are so young, however holy they were, for, when people have no experience, they will work great havoc, even with the best intentions.[2]

Teresa too had much to learn, and she learnt it the hard way – by trial and error – not visions.

Another personality connected with the Pastrana friars was Catherine of Cordona, one-time governess at the royal court who, in the caves of la Roda established herself as an anchorite and dressed like a man. From her retreat she contacted the friars and eventually received their habit while continuing to live in highly bizarre manner. A transvestite, locally revered, scattering blessings as she passed, too self-willed to wear the garb of a nun, excited plenty of comment. Teresa knew of the lady by hearsay and wondered if she should emulate her in mortification. She was duly reassured by a heavenly voice "...Seest thou the life of great penitence she lives? I value thy obedience more".[3] Most likely the 'voice' was Teresa's subconscious protest against such excesses – she always distrusted the flamboyant and valued what was balanced and humane. In fact it is in contrast to other contemporary so-called 'saints' that she stands out as one formed in the school of the Gospel. In Pastrana, her nuns too, under their high-handed benefactress the Princess of Eboli, rode out many a storm. Eventually the convent had to be transferred elsewhere when the Princess, on the death of her husband, insisted on trying her vocation to the cloister, but only obeyed the rules which suited her.

Each new foundation had its own history, its own troubles, and the cares of office kept Teresa alert from five in the morning, when she rose for her first hour of prayer, until well after Matins when she retired to her cell to catch up on correspondence. There were patrons to be placated, city permissions to be sought, churchmen to pacify, quarrels to circumvent when *conversos* wished to establish and endow monasteries – a privilege which had formerly been reserved to the nobility. At Toledo this last was almost certainly the case, and the Carmel materialised in the shadow of the great synagogue where perhaps Teresa's grandfather Sanchez had worshipped in his youth.

At this period Teresa was continually on the road, dealing with princesses and paupers in the same forthright manner. At Toledo, where the Archbishop of Spain's primatial see was in the custody of the Inquisition as a result of theological jealousies and manoevres for power, she was having difficulty in getting her way. As the Archbishop was 'unavailable' (actually a prisoner of the heretic hunters) and no one wanted to give her the necessary documents, she went and harangued the Cathedral administrator:

When I saw him I told him that it was hard that there should be women anxious to live in such austerity and perfection, and strictly enclosed, while those who had never done any such thing themselves but were living a comfortable life should try to hinder work which was of such service to the Lord. I told him all this and a good deal more, speaking with a resoluteness with which I was inspired by the Lord. This touched his heart and before I left he gave me the licence.[4]

This can stand as one example of how Teresa went about her business, leaving the powerful shamefaced before her enthusiasm for God. On the personal level however she was wholly gracious and gratetul for the smallest gift.

The grace of the Holy Spirit be with you (she wrote to a Toledan benefactress) and preserve you for the trouble you have gone to in sending me presents. The butter was delicious, as I should have expected it to be, coming from you, and as everything is that you send me. I shall accept it in the hope that if you have any more nice butter you will remember me again for it does me a lot of good. The quince cheese was delicious too: really, you seem to think of nothing but making me happy.[5]

As for her nuns, Teresa knew how to lighten the hardships inherent in beginnings which involved real privation and insecurity. At these times her humour was strongly in evidence. The house is small? Well:

However large the house may be what benefit is that to us? We can only make use of a single cell – what do we gain by its being large and well built? What indeed! We have not to spend all our time looking at the walls.[6]

There are no material comforts? Not so much as a "scrap of brushwood on which to boil a sardine?"[7] Then all the better for contemplation. Lack of outer amenities brings inner spiritual joy! At Salamanca she had the foresight of experience to see that at least straw was provided beforehand for bedding; but her timid companion was too afraid to sleep lest the two be molested during the night by students who had had to vacate the building. Teresa only laughed. "Well, sister, I shall consider what to do if the occasion arises" said she stretching out on the straw. Then she adds for the benefit of her readers, "as we had had two bad nights, sleep soon drove away our fears".[8]

As foundress, Teresa was thoroughly maternal in her role. All her geese were swans and she saw the sisters and friars through the glow of a mother's eyes. Later experience was to make her more wary, but to the end she put a good construction on even the most outrageous behaviour. She just could not believe others were not as sincere and upright as herself. With such a loving heart she was bound to be hurt. So many whom she lauds in her *Book of Foundations* proved to be sad disappointments. There was the beautiful and headstrong Casilda de Padilla who spurned her fiancé and forced her way into the Valladolid Carmel at the age of twelve,[9] only to leave it to become abbess of a wealthy franciscan house when she was seventeen. There was Mariano, the erstwhile hermit, who made much trouble by his tactless handling of the Order's business.[10] There was Doria whom she judged to be "so full of virtue" that she "praised our Lord for having given the Order a person like that".[11] She thought him chosen by God and entirely trustworthy yet, on gaining power after her death he almost destroyed the Teresian Reform by his insistence on rigid observance. "The religious are God's servants, not rogues or galley slaves" cried his opponent Gracian, objecting to Doria's harsh legislation. His reward – expulsion from the Discalced; the very man in whom Teresa had placed her hopes and with whom she was linked by a most intimate friendship.

In Teresa's writings we gain an insight into the lives of Spanish women – their lack of free choice regarding vocation and their often horrific childhoods. No wonder she devotes a full chapter of the *Foundations* to the treatment of 'melancholy' which at that time was a blanket word covering more or less everything from headstrong behaviour to endogenous depression. The childhood of a certain "Beatriz, daughter of most Christian parents" (was Teresa writing with her tongue in her cheek?) reads like a present day chronicle of child abuse. The poor girl was falsely accused of murder, whipped, tortured and made to sleep on the floor. When she reached puberty and refused to accept the husband selected for her by these same "most Christian parents" they "beat her and inflicted such treatment on her (even throttling her and trying to strangle her) that it was only by good luck they did not kill her. But God who needed her for other purposes spared her life".[12]

Not surprisingly, young women with such a background did not adjust easily to the pressures of life in an enclosed convent and needed great tenderness and understanding as they struggled with their handicap, for "we never quite become saints in this life,"[13] so "one must deal with people according to their temperament".[14] Neither need we be surprised that Teresa had her quota of 'failures' even though she tried to attract the best type of woman to her houses. Despite pressures she stood out against accepting people just because they could supply a dowry or had the backing of an esteemed benefactress, as the following letter shows:

I do beg your Ladyship to consider the matter carefully... If the house were one with a great number of people a defect here or there might pass muster but, when there are few, it stands to reason they must be carefully chosen... So my own feeling is that neither of the two applicants should be accepted, for I can see nothing in them that would benefit the house neither sanctity nor merit nor talent, nor exceptional discretion. If they would harm the convent why does your Ladyship wish to have them?... In your house every nun who is admitted ought to be good enough to be prioress or to hold any office for which she might he needed... Remember that we must always aim at the good of all.[15]

In Teresa's concern for her convents no detail was over-looked. If while at St Joseph's she had wished for two hands to write with at once, when it came to practical work she must have wished for four! Her prayer time was eaten into supervising workmen, drawing up plans, instructing her sisters, managing money with an astute business sense.

People have such blind confidence in me (she wrote to her favourite brother, Lorenzo) – I don't know how they can do these things, but they seem to trust me so implic-itly that they will give me as much as a thousand or two thousand ducats. So, although I used to detest money and business matters, it is the Lord's pleasure that I should engage in nothing else, and that is no light cross. May His Majesty grant me to serve him in this, for everything will pass away.[16]

In the midst of these distractions Teresa never forgot that 'those given her by the Father' were the most precious assets of the Reform. With all her experience of religious life she was eager that young prioresses be helped to gov-ern wisely and not attempt such excesses as had prevailed at Alcala. The Rule alone was enough without any addi-tional impositions and 'pet devotions'. She wanted her prioresses to be women of stature, strong and compassion-ate as she was; many indeed were to become fine foundresses and spiritual guides in their own right – Anne of Jesus (Lobera), Mary of St Joseph (Salazar), Anne of St Bartholomew (her lay-sister infirmarian and amanuensis) to mention but a few. And to all her nuns she was friend, teacher, leader, mother, though she also knew how to be stern:

I am annoyed at the way the prioress is fasting. Tell her so: I don't want to write myself or have anything to do with her for that very reason. God preserve me from people who would rather have their own way than do as they are told.[17]

When it came to formation Teresa eschewed the harsh methods then in vogue in other reformed Orders. She wrote in her own *Constitutions*:

Let the novice mistress treat the novices compassionately and lovingly. She must not be surprised at their faults for their progress is bound to be gradual. She shall exercise them in mortification according to what each one is able to take, attaching more importance to their not failing in virtue than to severity in penance.[18]

A life of prayer, she well saw, did not depend on outward rigour which could be mere conformity. To be a prayer one needed an upright heart and a pure conscience. Any pretentiousness or posturing as a saint she abhored. She remembered three women who "were saints in their own estimation" but when she got to know them they "frightened me more than all the sinners I have ever met". Upon which she exclaims "Let us beseech the Lord to enlighten us!"[19] While Teresa shared her responsibilities in those early years she never abdicated her authority. She was convinced she was doing God's work and he would call her to account for it. Bad health or spiritual trials deterred her not at all. "You must realise that in the spiritual world as in this world there are different kinds of weather"[20] she wrote to a layman friend. This was nothing to worry about and the only solution was to carry on regardless.

At the beginning of 1571 Teresa was fully immersed in her work as foundress: negotiating for suitable houses, seeing to relocation if sites proved unhealthy, palliating irate relatives over the deposition of dowries or the granting of patronage rights. She always tried to see the overall picture and was annoyed at a narrow vision:

...It is a great mistake to think you know everything and then say you are humble. You do not look beyond the limits of your own small house, whereas you should be considering what is most important for the houses as a whole. To do that is to lay the foundations of unrest and to bring everything toppling to the ground... I cannot think where you get so much vanity from to give you all that rashness...[21]

Moving back and forth between her convents Teresa was jealous of her sisters' right to live as they had vowed. It was at this juncture that the Carmelite Provincial, Fr Angel de Salazar, tried to impose a prioress of his own choice upon the Medina Carmel. His protegée was Teresa de Quesada who had joined the Reform from the Incarnation. Teresa was indignant. Her nuns had the right to vote for their own prioress, and anyway she did not consider the Provincial's choice a wise one. Nevertheless she was obliged to depart from Medina in the middle of winter, undertaking the long, cold journey back to St Joseph's in Avila while leaving the convent to its fate.

Teresa's fears did not prove groundless. Her namesake, unable to cope with the resentful Medina community, returned to the Incarnation and the mitigated Rule and Teresa was bidden to replace her and restore order. It was here that the unexpected summons arrived recalling her to the Incarnation. The Provincial, together with the Apostolic Visitor, had decided the house was in dire need of proper government; what better choice could there be than *La Madre*? Also, in this way the sly Provincial could remove her from her work with the Reform which was spreading fast among both men and women. In a definite job she could be more adequately supervised – or so he thought.

Teresa reacted with dismay. She was being asked to restore some semblance of religious discipline to a house that did not want her. What was happening to her was exactly what had transpired at Medina but in reverse. A prioress was to be imposed without the vote of the majority behind her. It was a perilous undertaking. Maybe she would fail at the Incarnation as Teresa de Quesada had failed at Medina? Her one comfort was that she was allowed to formally renounce the mitigated Rule, while being proclaimed officially a nun, not of the Incarnation, but of the Salamanca discalced community.

Her own nuns needed her guidance, love and support as they struggled to stabilise themselves in their respective cities, and here was Teresa being forbidden the continual contact with them that she was used to and felt they needed. However, she had no option but to accept her appointment. On July 10th 1571 she was declared Prioress of the Incarnation and on October 6th of that year she was to take up residence in the convent she had left nine years previously, thinking she would never return.

NOTES

1. *Foundations*, ch. 14.
2. *Letter*, 295.
3. *Relations*, no. 23.
4. *Foundations*, ch. 15.
5. *Letter*, 23.
6. *Foundations*, ch. 14.
7. *Foundations*, ch. 15.
8. *Foundations*, ch. 19.
9. Cf *Foundations*, ch. 10 and 11. These chapters were omitted from the published book for many years as they betray Teresa's gullibility and misjudgement.
10. See for example *Letter*, 121.
11. *Letter*, 281.
12. *Foundations*, ch. 26.
13. *Letter*, 124.
14. *Letter*, 56.
15. *Letter*, 34.
16. *Letter*, 19.
17. *Letter*, 39.
18. *Primitive Constitutions*, no. 40 (Order's official translation).
19. *Conceptions*, ch. 2.
20. *Letter*, 66.
21. *Letter*, 78a.

Prioress of the Incarnation

Interlude in Avila and foundation at Segovia. 1571-74

If Teresa's resourcefulness and tact had been needed in superabundance for her own foundations, they were needed even more as she prepared to face a hostile community. She was not going to the Incarnation as a much loved mother and spiritual guide but as an 'outsider' imposed from above when the sisters felt they had a right to elect whomsoever they chose. This was no easy assignment and Teresa might have been forgiven had she merely accepted it as a formality while continuing to give her time, money and energy to her own convents. But this was not her way. Perhaps nowhere else do we see her character so clearly delineated to the good as during these years at her *alma mater*.

Her reintroduction to the community was certainly inauspicious. Teresa was escorted from St Joseph's and through the city gates by three Carmelite ecclesiastics and several officers of the law. Trouble was in the air and force might be required before the new prioress was installed. The procession made its way across the plain towards the convent, swelled by the usual crowd of hangers-on and curious folk who hoped to witness a bit of excitement. It was common knowledge that Teresa had demanded in advance that all secular persons leave the precincts. She intended to be superior of the sisters certainly, but had no intention of trying to impose her wishes on residents not bound by a vow of obedience.

What would become of the Incarnation under this new regime wondered the townsfolk as they tagged along after the cross-bearer and the elderly nun in a patched habit, her white mantle held close to keep out the autumn chill, seem-

101

ingly oblivious to the fact that she was the focus of attention.

The nuns of the Incarnation were waiting for her, determined to resist. Teresa had been one of themselves for more than twenty years before leaving to commence a stricter form of life. This seemed an implicit criticism which they could scarcely tolerate. Besides, many of the best and most promising of their number had actually joined the Reform and were now in Discalced convents. The Provincial might have the authority to demand their submission but he, after all, was not being asked to live under Teresa's government which, they thought, was bound to be repressive. The women were adamant. Their voice of protest would be heard even if their actions proved ineffectual.

When Teresa's party arrived outside the church pandemonium issued from within the enclosure. The stoutest nuns tried to block the entrance, others shrieked and shook their fists defiantly, one fainted in the crush. A small faction who wanted their new prioress intoned the *Te Deum* above the noise. Teresa quietly passed through the hubbub and knelt before the altar in the choir. There was something in her presence which demanded respect. In the midst of such a debacle she at least would show the Lord reverence in his own house.

Having seen Teresa enter the men retired, thankful that their reception had been no worse. The curious onlookers saw the door shut and regretted that the spectacle had not been more prolonged and entertaining. Well, let the nuns get on with their own lives, time would tell whether or not Mother Teresa of Jesus could do anything with them. Inside the enclosure however she was already winning hearts as, disregarding the opposition, she spoke gently to the overexcited and hysterical. Her calm, deliberate movements restored a sense of order and decency. Then she went quietly to her cell to prepare for the morrow when she would be expected to address the Chapter sisters at the beginning of her period of government.

She initiated her priorate with an act which can be

deemed a stroke of genius. It showed how well Teresa understood the human heart – more weak than sinful, only waiting tor a touch of kindness and a hand reaching out in trust not condemnation. She instinctively fathomed what would ease a difficult situation and heal wounds that would otherwise fester beneath the surface. As the sisters gathered in their choir that October day, possibly October 7th 1571, the very day that the Christian forces won a decisive victory at the battle of Lepanto and saved Europe from the Turks, Teresa won her own personal victory over her new community.

The nuns turned towards the prioress's stall for the inauguration of their superior, but there stood, not Teresa, but the beautiful image of Our Lady of Clemency, holding in her hands the keys of the convent. At her feet on the floor sat the prioress, her feet tucked neatly under her habit as was the custom among the Discalced. The symbolism was obvious – the Virgin, not Teresa, was to be the real guide of the community. Meanwhile she began her opening speech:

Ladies, mothers and my sisters... I come only to serve you and to administer to your pleasure as far as I am able; and to this end I hope the Lord will help me greatly. For as to the rest any one of you can teach and reform me. For that reason consider my ladies, that what I can do for each one of you I will do willingly, even to the shedding of blood and giving up my life. I am a daughter of this house and a sister of your graces. I know the circumstances and necessities of all, or of the greater number; there is no reason to dread one who is so entirely yours. Do not fear my rule, for although I have lived until now, and ruled among Discalced nuns, by the Lord's mercy I know well how those who are not should be governed. My desire is that we should all serve our Lord with suavity; and that we should do the little enjoined on us by our Rule and Constitutions, for love of the Lord to whom we owe so much. Well do I

103

know how great is our weakness, but although our works do not reach so far let our desires do so; for the Lord is pitiful and will order it so that, little by little, our works shall rise to our intentions and desires.[1]

Perhaps the words preserved are apocryphal but their tone and sweetness are certainly *La Madre*'s and similar sentiments abound in her writings. The nuns were mollified, and most were won to her side.

Ever since that memorable day Our Lady of Clemency has reigned from the centre of the choir at the Incarnation, and in all Discalced houses up to the present the place usually reserved for the prioress in a monastic church has been given to a statue of the Virgin, who presides as honorary mistress.

Later, on the eve of St Sebastian's feast, January 19th the following year, Teresa had one of her most touching visions located in the same choir stall and recorded for posterity in her *Relations*. It took place during the singing of the *Salve Regina* at the end of the day:

I saw the Mother of God descend to the prioress's stall where Our Lady is enthroned and seat herself there... Our Lady remained there during the whole of the *Salve* and said to me "You have done well to place me here; I will be here when praises are offered to my Son and will present them to him". After that I remained in the state of prayer which I experience when my soul is in the company of the Most Holy Trinity; and I thought the Person of the Father drew me to himself and spoke words which were most comfortable. Among them were these, which showed me the love he had for me: "I gave you my Son and the Holy Spirit and this Virgin. What can you give me?"[2]

The desire to give God everything was basic to Teresa's whole spirituality. She could not understand how, when God had given so much, we could be content with giving only a little in return. And the Incarnation was testing her generosity towards God: her giving was not painless. To her friend Dona Luisa she confided:

> May Our Lord reward your Ladyship for your kind letter, which was a great comfort to me – and I can tell you I needed it! Oh, my Lady, to have experienced the tranquillity of our (Discalced) houses, and then to find oneself in this hurlyburly! I don't know how anyone can live here at all. However, there is always something to try us everywhere! And, glory be to God, there is peace here now – that is something![3]

On the practical level Teresa was extremely active in her post. Part of the trouble at the Incarnation was its extreme poverty owing to the mismanagement of funds and the custom of each providing for herself. Energetically Teresa tried to raise money and thus restore a level of observance that at least meant all could eat. "Send me the turkeys, as you have so many"[4] she begged Juana, and she diverted money given for her own foundations to provide food for her present community. For herself, she subsisted on the gifts of wellwishers and only took her bread from the convent supplies, lest she be considered a financial drain on the Incarnation's meagre resources. Another move was to close the parlours, at least for the Lenten season, and discourage the frequent comings and goings of nuns and visitors. She did all this so tactfully, ever respectful of the sisters' dignity, that soon even the most rebellious were subdued and tractable. She loved the sick, having made a special point in her own Constitutions that they be treated with "the greatest love, indulgence and compassion".[5] This continued at the Incarnation and she was assiduous in procuring necessities for them[6] and insisting on cleanliness in beds and linen "at whatever cost: it is terrible not to have that".[7]

Even so, Teresa felt extremely lonely in her position and her health suffered. She mentions pains, fever, being bled and purged, an attack of quinsy and faceache.[8] "I miss you here and feel much alone" she penned to her sister Juana, and expressed surprise at how she managed to keep going with her burden of cares – not just regarding the Incarnation but the additional pressure of worries about her own foundations.[9] In after years, when a nun from a large community wished to join Teresa's Reform she dissuaded her with the following advice, revealing how convinced she was that loving God does not require other and special circumstances but rather an acceptance of our own, as and where we are:

> Before the first of these convents of ours was founded, I spent twenty-five years in one in which there were a hundred and eighty nuns. And as I am writing in a hurry I will only say that to anyone who loves God all such things will be a cross and thus will bring profit to the soul. They will be powerless to harm it if, whatever you are doing, you bear in mind that you are alone in the house with God... Try to cultivate the virtue that you see in each of the nuns, love her for that virtue, profit by it, and pay no attention to her faults... for, after all, my Lady, we can love this great God wherever we are.[10]

To ameliorate her isolation and aid the sisters in their spiritual growth Teresa recognised a need for good directors. The Carmelite fathers of Avila might be good enough men in themselves but they had proved ineffectual as spiritual guides – that much was obvious. Teresa therefore decided to bring John of the Cross to Avila as confessor to the nuns. He had exceptional gifts of discernment; the fact that nearly all his deep friendships were with women testified to his insight and compassion in their regard. He and a companion friar were installed first in the Calced friary in the city and then, when difficulties arose with the brethren, in two workmen's huts just outside the enclosure. Like Teresa, his care for the sisters did not extend only to their souls. When he noticed a nun without shoes simply because she had no money to buy any he begged sufficient alms for their purchase. When an extra treat was sent out on his tray for a feastday he would send it to one of the sick sisters in the infirmary, knowing that the convent could provide little in the way of comforts.

With two such Carmelites in charge the Incarnation was soon, if not a model of regular observance, at least vastly improved. This meant Teresa could turn her attention to her own convents for a while. The ecclesiastical superiors wanted her immured at the Incarnation, she felt her other houses needed her too. The men insisted on enclosure and stability, she felt the exigencies of the moment should take precedence. So, when permission to travel was unforthcoming, she took the matter into her own hands and appealed to the King via a special messenger.[11] Philip II immediately granted her request.

Having attended to necessary business in Alba she proceeded after a short interval to Salamanca and while there received unexpected permission to make a new foundation in Segovia. She was on the road once more – the Provincial bowed before the designs of Providence. Teresa was 'gadding about' again!

The foundress had good friends resident in Segovia and other good friends who eased the long journey for her when she eventually set out, John of the Cross accompanying her. Once a house had been obtained in the face of the usual difficulties "which involved us in several law suits" for having to placate other religious communities in the vicinity "this time the Mecedarians and the Cathedral Chapter", she exclaimed in bewilderment, "Oh Jesus, how troublesome it is to have to contend with such a variety of opinions. Writing about it doesn't seem much, but going through it was plenty of trouble!"[12] To the Segovian convent Teresa brought her nuns from Pastrana, literally fleeing from the outrageous behaviour of the Princess of Eboli.

With Segovia established Teresa must certainly have been feeling her age. She was approaching sixty, old for a woman of the Renaissance period, and one constantly on the move. Increasing infirmities pressed on her. Several of her early companions had died young; others, though still young in years, bore the weight of maturity in governing and relied on Teresa for encouragement and advice.

> I am distressed to think what a great trial this long business must have been for you my daughter (she wrote to the twenty-eight year old prioress of Valladolid) it is most troublesome I know what it means.[13] But I think your health would get worse rather than better if you had the period of quietness you speak of. I feel sure of that because I know your temperament, and I can endure seeing you bear trials, for you would be a saint in any case, and these desires which you have for solitude are better for you than the solitude itself would be.[14]

Teresa returned to Avila in time to complete her three year term as prioress and hand over her office to a successor, leaving the Incarnation on a reasonably sure financial as well as spiritual footing. She then retired to St Joseph's for a rest, brief though it proved to be. Here in her first convent, in the midst of loving daughters, she was at peace. Her foundations were prospering, she was venerated by a concourse of friends and well-wishers. She deserved a respite as age made inroads upon her health and good looks. Already her body was heavy and she leaned often upon a staff. But rest was not for her. She spent Christmas at Valladolid seeing to the business of Casilda's dowry that had so depressed Mother Maria Bautista. At the festival, with her daughters around her she danced and sang while they played the castanets, pipes and drums for the little King:

> I heard a sound as of faintest music:
> Seem'd they were singing a snatch of song.
> "Bras, let us visit the shepherd-maiden:
> Dawn is showing and night is gone".
> "My shepherd-boy, go, see who's calling."
> " 'Tis angels, and the day is dawning."[15]

It was a warm-hearted family gathering – prelude to a year of trials of all kinds. "We must have great courage and never rest until we reach the end of the journey"[16] she had stated in the *Way of Perfection*; and in the *Interior Castle* she was to write at a future date:

If (a person's) mind is fixed on God as it ought to be, she must needs forget herself, all her thoughts are bent on how to please him better and how she can show the love she bears him... If you love you will never be content to come to a standstill.[17]

And in this as always Teresa lived as she taught.

NOTES

1. The text of the address is found in the *Appendix* to the *Complete Works*. This translation is from *Santa Teresa*, by G. Cunninghame Graham.
2. *Relations*, no. 25.
3. *Letter*, 31.
4. *Letter*, 36.
5. *Primitive Constitutions*, no. 23.
6. Cf *Letter*, 31.
7. *Letter*, 350.
8. *Letter*, 33.
9. Cf *Letter*, 31.
10. *Letter*, 363.
11. Cf *Letter*, 45.
12. *Foundations*, ch. 21 (Kavanaugh translation).
13. The reference is to trouble in arranging for the deposition of the dowry of Sr Casilda, the twelve-year-old who had entered the Valladolid Carmel and whose noble relatives did not wish to see their money swallowed up in a convent. Casilda later left the Carmel for a Franciscan Abbey – a great embarrassment to Teresa.
14. *Letter*, 53.
15. *Poems*, 14.
16. *Way of Perfection*, ch. 21.
17. *Interior Castle*, Mansion 7, ch. 4 (Stanbrook translation).

Beas and beloved Gratian

Teresa travels farther afield. 1575

In January 1575 Teresa planned a comprehensive itinerary during which she hoped to visit a number of her convents and establish a new house of Discalced nuns at Beas de Segura. Beas was the furthest South she had ventured – she even wondered whether it was still within the confines of Castile as she had no permission to spread her Reform beyond that. She hesitated, despite being assured of the beauty of the place and its healthful climate. To her, Beas might as well be at the other side of the world.

Meanwhile in that town two *beatas*, Catherine and Maria Godinez, begged Teresa to undertake the journey, as their parents were now dead and they had resolved to devote their patrimony to the founding of a Carmelite convent. In recounting the story of Catherine, the eldest of the two, Teresa gives us another fascinating glimpse into the religious climate of the time and the struggle for women to choose their own manner of life.

At fourteen, Catherine de Sandoval, daughter of wealthy and influential parents, underwent a sudden conversion. Earlier she had shown remarkable spirit in refusing several offers of marriage, considering no man her equal because "my intention is for my descendants to take their rise from *me*". Teresa adds that the girl "had no inclination to be married for she thought it demeaning to be subject to anyone, and she had no idea whence this pride came. The Lord knew how it could be cured, blessed be his mercy!"[1] The perfectly natural desire to avoid a possibly chattel-like relationship (where money and connections counted for more than mutual love) was taken to be a vice even by Teresa, though she may only have been indulging in currently approved sentiments.

The sight of an inscription over a crucifix changed Catherine's heart, and she resolved henceforward to humble herself and become like the Lord. All her desires for independence were transformed into a longing for suffering, penance and humiliations – though it is worth noting that these yearnings for the cross did *not* include a husband. The independent Catherine de Sandoval would rather be subject only to the King of Heaven!

As the girl's parents refused consent to her becoming a nun, Catherine, after three years pleading, assumed the habit of a *beata* (a plain dress signifying a life of devotion), to be followed shortly by her sister Maria. The two then gave themselves to prayer, penance and charitable works while still remaining at home. When an attempt to teach little girls failed the sisters seem to have retreated into a series of illnesses – a psychosomatic protest no doubt against the restrictions they were continually facing. At length, both parents having died, they were free to endow a convent in the hope of entering it themselves. They had spent over twenty years in a limbo of unfulfilled desires.

As Beas was a town belonging to the Knights of Santiago the obtaining of a license for founding had scant hope of success tor "there were people who had spent years in trying to obtain permission from them".[2] But Catherine had made up her mind. An indication of her determination to succeed was her promise that if the Lord restored her health within a month it could surely be taken as a sign to her opponents that God wished the foundation to be made. Teresa made her own assessment of the situation, commenting:

At the time (Catherine) said this she had not left her bed for over six months, and had hardly been able to stir from it for eight. For eight years she had suffered from continual fever, together with consumption and dropsy: she also had a burning fire in the liver which was so violent that the heat could be felt through the bedclothes and burned her nightgown. This seems incredible, but I

111

heard it from the physician who was attending her at the time and it completely astounded me. She also had rheumatic gout and sciatica.[3]

Teresa adds further macabre details about continual bloodletting and cancer treatment which make it sound as if the pious *beata* was more properly a candidate for a terminal hospice than a reformed, penitential convent. But the latter option seemed infinitely preferable to continued misery 'in the world' and Catherine received a sudden cure for all her maladies. The prospect of a convent aroused hope within her and hope is the greatest of all miracle workers.

The gullible were suitably impressed by the invalid's rapid return to health. She forthwith travelled to Madrid and there, like the importunate widow of the Gospels, persevered in her petition until she received the King's permission to found as she wished. He was personally an admirer of the Discalced and wished to see the Reform extended. Such an intrepid woman could not help but impress Teresa, who had certainly not expected a license to be obtained. Nor had the Carmelite Provincial, who had allowed her to acquiesce to Catherine's initial pleas because he was certain a license would be refused. Little did he understand the women with whom he was dealing!

It was a long journey to Beas and it followed on a tour of several of Teresa's other foundations – Segovia, Toledo and Malagon. From Malagon she set out with quite a large party as if for an important expedition – as indeed to her it was. She took with her to those distant parts some of her best nuns, with the indomitable Fr Julian, a layman Antonio Gaytan (whose seven year old little daughter was allowed to be received in the Carmel of Alba) and a secular priest to whom Teresa was to give the habit and the name Fr Gregorio Nazianzen.

Their path took them South, right to the borders of Andalusia, Teresa and her sisters having to cope with all the inconveniences of bad inns, bad weather, and the minimum of comfort. The foundress was known for her good humour at these times and her quick repartee. On one occasion she assured her travelling companions that the difficulties of the journey gave them rich opportunities for winning heaven. To which one wag smartly retorted "But I was winning heaven just as much at home!"[4]

The covered carts, with their occupants swaying to the rhythm of mules and wheels crossed the muddy, rutted plains of La Mancha and negotiated the majestic passes of the Serra Morena which divide Andalusia from Castile. In these precipitous heights they lost their way, only to be warned of possible danger by a wandering shepherd who, hidden by the steep terrain, shouted into the void. As he remained invisible Teresa immediately attributed the escape from danger to her good friend St Joseph. Her intimacy with this saint never diminished. He was to her an untiring friend and companion on all her travels and his name graced many of her convents, including the one at Beas which became "the Carmel of the glorious St Joseph of the Saviour".

At last the travellers found themselves looking down over the town, which lay before them amid the tranquillity of vineyards and olive groves, so different from the arid splendour of Teresa's native province. She was now among different people. How would she fare with them? She need not have worried; there was a welcome awaiting her like none other.

Teresa's entry into Beas was the first of those triumphal processions which were to be repeated in Palencia, Soria, Villeneuva de la Jara and belatedly in Seville and Burgos. The days when she had to sneak into a house and establish herself under cover of darkness were over. As she approached the town a group of knights rode out to escort the wagons, followed by a gaggle of eager peasants anxious to see *la Santa*, the foundress. Church bells pealed a greeting amid shouts of joy and acclaim for Spain's "great old lady". Some dropped to their knees to seek her blessing. Clergy on the steps of the parish church waited nervously

113

and self-consciously as the first cart rolled forward and from it descended the heavily veiled Teresa leaning on a stick. She was followed by her sisters, each one veiled over the face like a Moorish bride, each weary from the long journey.

Almost immediately a procession formed behind the cross and strains of the *Te Deum* pierced the February mildness. Past the jubilant townsfolk, through the narrow streets festooned with bunting and flowers, Teresa made her way to the place where the Godinez sisters awaited her. A 'saint' was gracing Beas with her presence and the citizens wanted to rejoice publicly at their good fortune. Teresa was oblivious of it all. She was tired. Her one wish was to enter an enclosure and get some rest among 'her own'. She set about finalising arrangements and within a month gave the habit to the two women who had worked so relentlessly for her advent. Catherine's health continued to improve when she became a nun while her younger sister Maria in due course was elected Prioress of the Beas Carmel.

In the flurry of organising the new foundation, together with the general rejoicing that accompanied it, Teresa was thrown off guard by unforseen complications. She discovered that while geographically Beas was in Castile (on the borders of the Kingdom of Toledo) ecclesiastically it was in a diocese of Andalusia where she had no permission to establish the Discalced. Trouble was to ensue. Old and ailing as she was, Teresa would recover her strength to do battle for the defence of the Reform to which she had dedicated her life and which was now on the verge of disintegration. On the one hand many admired her; on the other were those jealous of her influence who threatened to destroy all she had initiated at such cost.

At Beas Teresa was to meet the young man destined to influence her most profoundly during the years of life left to her; one upon whom she pinned her highest hopes for the future of the Order – Fr Jerome of the Mother of God (Gratian). Together they would face the storm of persecution, together uphold one another with genuine love and affirmation when times were difficult. In Gratian (strange that for him as for his protagonist, Nicholas Doria, he is remembered in history by his family rather than his religious name), Teresa felt she had found a true soul-friend. He was gifted, fluent, spiritual, filled with ardour for the cause of the Discalced. While she lived, Teresa and Gratian in unison steered the Reform through its years of turmoil; when she died, those who hated her protegée hounded him from the Order to disgrace and exile. Already these forces were at work beneath the surface. The power game can be as rife in religious Orders as anywhere else, and there are always people ready to play it for the highest stakes.

Jerome Gratian at this time was a young friar of twenty-eight who had risen rapidly to eminence and was presently Visitator of the men's branch of the Carmelite Order in Andalusia. He was a son of the humanist secretary of King Philip II, with a mother, Doña Juana Dantisco, of Polish origin; one of twenty brothers and sisters, all of them distinguished and refined in education and upbringing. Jerome himself was exceptionally gifted on both the intellectual and personal level, as was Teresa, and when he entered the newly established Discalced noviciate at Pastrana he was considered a real 'catch'. His presence was imposing (though like John of the Cross he was prematurely bald) and his preaching had all the passion of Tridentine oratorical display.

The attraction of the sixty year old Teresa to the younger man was not purely spiritual, as seems to have been the case between her and John of the Cross (as far as any friendship can be classed as 'spiritual' divorced from 'natural'). Here on the contrary was the pull of *eros* – two people irresistibly drawn together in love and understanding, a natural sympathy and affection that strikes deep roots when it is present and makes short work of the usual longdrawn-out preliminaries of friendship when men and women are engaged in a similar project but feel no special mutual attraction. With Teresa and Gratian the barriers were down almost immediately as they discussed the Reform and its future. "She revealed her spirit to me without any reservation, and I did likewise with her. We agreed there and then to proceed in complete agreement in all our undertakings. Furthermore, she took a particular vow of obedience to me, over and above her normal religious vow", wrote Gratian as he recalled that day of destiny. There was too no doubt an element of transference in this. Teresa was the mother, Gratian the beloved son who mirrored the Son of the Father to whom she was espoused. And why not? Are the saints immune from the natural processes of growth, psychological no less than spiritual and physical?

In her joy Teresa wrote to the prioress of Medina del Campo:

Oh Mother, how much I wished you were with me during these last few days! I must tell you without exaggeration that I think they have been the best days of my life. For over three weeks we have had Father-Master Gratian here, and much as I have had to do with him, I assure you I have not yet fully realised his worth. To me he is perfect, and better for our needs than anyone else we could have asked God to send us. What your reverence and all the nuns must do now is to beg His Majesty to give him to us as superior. If that happens, I can take a rest from governing these houses, for anyone so perfect and yet so gentle I have never seen. May God have him in his keeping and preserve him; I would not have missed seeing him and having to do with him for anything in the world.[5]

Teresa had much to say on detachment but her humanity was too warm, too genuine, to be held back by rigid convention. If she loved she loved with the whole of herself, and as this left her vulnerable so it broke her open in compassion for others. Her one reservation was that those she loved must also be lovers of God, for having "seen the beauty of the Lord" nothing and nobody else could dominate her heart exclusively.

116

Gratian suggested, nay commanded, that Teresa make another foundation, this time in Seville, deep in Andalusia. Having taken him as her director she obeyed, thinking that the General's prohibition of Andalusian foundations could no longer apply. In the fierce summer heat she gathered those she had chosen for the convent and set out. She was travelling to a new city, a new province, and a new stage in the history of the Reform, though at the time she knew it not.

NOTES

1. *Foundations*, ch. 22.
2. Ibid.
3. Ibid.
4. Testimony of Mother Mary of St Jerome, *op. cit.*
5. *Letter*, 72.
6. *Life*, ch. 37.

In Andalusia

The foundations of Seville and Caravaca.
Trouble with the General. 1575-76

It was a terrible journey. Teresa was prostrate with fever most of the way. The sun beat down – hotter than hell itself she thought, as she meditated on the verge of delirium.[1] Water was scarce, dearer than wine to purchase; fresh food was well nigh unattainable. The inns had never seemed so dirty nor the muleteers so quarrelsome. They nearly drowned when mooring ropes cut adrift and left them helpless on a raft, caught in the current of the Guadalquiver River. Fortunately they ran aground on a sandbank. Teresa was glad she had picked "courageous souls" [2]from her nuns for this foundation, for the trials of the journey proved negligible to those faced later, but with the group she had she felt so confident that "I think I would have ventured into the country of the Turks in their company".[3] At Cordoba where they halted en route, the nuns caused a great stir as they tried to enter a church inconspicuously to hear Mass. They found themselves instead in the midst of a crowd celebrating the Whitsun fiesta. Teresa was kicked aside unceremoniously and the group was received amidst such scenes of commotion that *La Madre*'s fever ceased from "the great shock".[4] The sight of the dark habits, white mantles and heavily veiled faces were enough to introduce uproar among the revellers gathered for Mass on the patronal feast of their church; but quite how Teresa expected their presence to pass unremarked is a mystery!

At the end of the trek there was no welcome, no house, no prospective novices, despite the fact they had been assured all was ready for their arrival. And the archbishop was hostile and refused a license. Oh Seville! What a welcome for Teresa, now old and tired and sick, at Spain's principal city and port of the Indies. She felt ready to turn back to Beas.

Of course she soon rallied and set about seeing to all that concerned the projected foundation. Her own indisposition counted for nothing if she thought she was forwarding God's work. She soldiered on in Seville planning, providing, winning people to her cause and also sent a contingent of nuns to Caravaca where another convent was inaugurated. But Teresa never really took to the Andalusians. She felt the sun had hardened them and its brightness reduced their souls to mere glitter.

It is amazing what injustices are committed in this part of the world (she wrote to Maria Bautista) what untruthfulness and double-dealing. I can assure you the place fully deserves its reputation. Blessed be the Lord who brings good out of everything. In spite of having so many troubles coming all at once I have felt a strange joy.[5]

The convent was eventually established amid scenes of revelry – a great procession, music and "a great many salvos of artillery were fired. Such grandeur was a delight to the spirit".[6] The Archbishop knelt publicly to ask her blessing; but none of this erased the painful memory of all Teresa had suffered for the foundation to be brought to fruition.

There were other problems too. Despite having picked some of her best sisters for the Seville convent it faced difficulties of a personal nature from the outset. Of those who entered, one *beata* who came to try her vocation denounced the community to the Inquisition. Teresa came under suspicion and the book of her *Life* was thoroughly perused lest it contain heresy. Another sister went insane and had to be forcibly restrained by stalwart infirmarians, a distressing situation in an enclosed convent to say the least. Two others spread scandalous rumours and dragged the nuns into a libel suit. Even the beloved prioress, Maria de San José, on this first Andalusian foray treated the foundress with contempt. Possibly she wanted to demonstrate her own capabilities and was impatient of the older woman taking such motherly care over all that needed to be done, while perhaps not being sufficiently sensitive to the desire of the younger Carmelite also to have her say. The difference was made up later thanks to Teresa's untiring affection. When she had left Seville and Maria de San José was feeling lonely, Teresa wrote to assure her that she was not forgotten and that her love for her remained unchanged:

Provided you love me as much as I love you, I forgive you everything, whether in the past or in the future. The chief complaint I have about you now is the little desire you had to be with me... whereas if you had wanted me I should have felt comforted... I count those trials as well suffered and should have been glad to suffer more of them if my doing so could have been of help to your Reverence and the sisters. For believe me, I have great affection for you and when I see you want me so much everything else is a mere trifle and not worth consideration, although at Seville where there was first one kind of trial and then another and I was treating you as one of my dearest daughters, it hurt me terribly not to find the same frankness and love in you. But this letter of yours has made me forget all that and only my desire for you remains now.[7]

So does a saint expose her emotions in trust and humility. One happy event during Teresa's sojourn in Seville was the return of two of her brothers from the Indies; Lorenzo her favourite, and Pedro (of melancholy temperament). Lorenzo, a widower and former mayor of Quito in Ecuador, brought his four children with him to be educated in Spain, and Teresa had the joy of being reunited with her loved ones. His little daughter Teresita immediately became the pet of her aged aunt who took her into the convent and dressed her in a diminutive habit – to the delight of her father and all the nuns who were charmed by her stories of the Americas. Teresita was to be inseparable from Teresa for the rest of her life, and it was on her way to Avila to receive her niece's profession that Teresa died. With characteristic zeal Teresa took Lorenzo's spiritual wellbeing seriously and wrote regular letters of advice. In one she gives directives about wearing a hairshirt – but it must be in moderation, and not at all if it affects the kidneys for "God prefers your health and your obedience to your penances... Don't do anything I tell you not to".[8] His *real* penance is coping with poor Pedro's melancholia, the rest is only an optional extra.

Tales of America and its native Indian population had prompted Teresa to expand her reform in the first place. She took a great interest in the new world and its riches, for thanks to the fortunes of *conquistadores* and their relatives many of her convents were put on a sound financial basis. She did not of course consider the social implications of conquest, the coercion, injustice, bloodshed... in this she could only be a woman of her time, but she certainly enjoyed the thought of this great land and the wonders it contained. Her eager intellect delighted in its many marvels – coconuts ("The sisters were delighted to see the coconuts and so was I. Blessed be he who created them: they are certainly something worth seeing"[9]), potatoes, medicines, perfumes... Her eyes followed the course of the galleys embarking for a destination beyond her experience but not beyond her prayer and concern. Foreigners had intrigued her since childhood and her projected martyrdom at the hand of the Moors. Now she was in a Moorish city which spoke of varied and rich cultures. Here she could just be herself – no one looked upon her as *la santa* in these parts as they did in Castile.

And one thing which makes me happy here, and will make me increasingly so, is that there is no suggestion of that nonsense about my supposed sanctity which people talked of in Castile. That allows me to live and go about without fear that ridiculous tower of their imagination would be falling down on top of me,[10]

she wrote jestlingly to the prioress of Vallodolid.

It was while Teresa tarried in Seville that matters in the Order came to a head and besides everything else she found herself trying to negotiate a way forward for her friars and nuns in the face of fierce opposition.

To put things very briefly: Teresa's aim had been to restore the Rule of St Albert without the accretion of mitigations, thus making it the basis for a reform movement within the Carmelite Order. Taking her cue from similar movements within other Orders she had inaugurated a 'barefooted' or Discalced branch which lived a stricter and more penitential life (not necessarily a 'holier' life) in contrast to the 'shod' or Calced friars and nuns of the mitigated or ordinary observance. There were very few Calced Carmelite nuns anyway and each house was autonomous, looking to nearby friars for spiritual guidance. Such had been the situation at the Incarnation in Avila. Teresa, in founding convents, had had a more or less free mandate to put her own ideas into practice. As the women were enclosed and dedicated to prayer difficulties were not immediately apparent. In fact the nuns were much admired.

The Discalced friars on the other hand were not so easily governed. Being men they had mobility for preaching and apostolic work and a degree of independence because of their priestly ministry. They were not officially an independent Order, merely a reformed branch within the wider Carmelite family. Friction was bound to be generated as vocations multiplied.

Rubeo, the General whom Teresa had met in Avila and who had authorised her to make more foundations, had stipulated that they must be confined to Castile. She had given herself to this work at cost to her health, travelling wherever it seemed there might be an opening for her nuns and proceeding only with the blessing of men in authority. However, on discovering that Beas was actually in Andalusia, and having made a vow of obedience to Gratian, she felt there could be no harm in proceeding to Seville at Gratian's urging. She put his command above the General's which naturally provoked the latter's wrath.

Parallel with this were difficulties among the friars. The number of the Discalced had increased and, being less influential than their Calced brethren, resorted to the weapons of the weak – duplicity and intrigue – to further their cause. Quarrels and ill-feeling erupted, exacerbated by the difficulties of communication between Rome and Spain. It might be recalled that Rubeo had come to Spain specifically to discipline the Carmelites and exhort them to a more perfect following of their vocation. He was not opposed to reform – that had been his ideal in the first place – but with his being so far away reports reached him in exaggerated guise. Men appointed to oversee the situation and mediate between the factions often appropriated greater authority to themselves than the situation warranted. They issued conflicting decrees according to where their personal sympathies lay, confirming their own favourites in office and threatening excommunication for the recalcitrant. The loudest, rather than the truest voices prevailed.

In Spain, the King tended to take the side of the Discalced (he wished to be "head of the Church" in his own domains every bit as much as Henry VIII in England) and Rome and the Order the side of the Calced. Gratian, a Discalced friar, as Visitor for Andalusia, was responsible for both Calced and Discalced Carmelites, each following a different interpretation of the Rule as far as practical application went, each claiming to be authentic inheritors of the Carmelite charism, each jealous of the other group, each struggling for supremacy. Teresa obviously felt the only answer was for the Discalced to become independent as far as internal government was concerned and she pleaded with the King for this – but to no avail. Deadlock ensued.

Meanwhile the fury of the Calced was aroused. They had already reported Teresa to the General for founding in Andalusia and he had demanded an explanation. She received his letter too late to exonerate herself in time, though her reply was an epistle of sincerity and charm. She truly loved the old man who had first sanctioned her Reform and his displeasure pained her deeply.

The letter went unheeded precisely because the governing body of the Order had already met in Rome and passed a resolution to suppress the Discalced friars and reintegrate them into the main body of Carmelites. Passions ran high on all sides and Gratian, for all his tact, found it impossible to act decisively at such a critical juncture. The trouble was that everyone seemed to have permission for what they were doing but each was appealing to a different authority! The way was neither clear cut nor unambiguous. The ambitious were mingled with the real seekers after truth, the powergrabbers with the humble. John of the Cross was spirited away to imprisonment and ill-treatment and even the King could not intervene despite Teresa's pleas.[11] The Discalced refused to yield and eventually, in March 1581, obtained their autonomy (though this was still in the future; the outcome at this time was far from assured).

Rubeo sent a decree ordering Teresa to refrain from founding any more convents and retire to a Carmel of her choice. She chose Toledo, where she would be closer to Gratian and thus be enabled to monitor the moves of her beloved "Eliseus" or "Paul" as she liked to call him – partly from affection, partly to ensure confidentiality should their correspondence be intercepted.

Teresa wrote once more to the General protesting her and her friars' loyalty to him despite reports he might have received asserting the contrary. Their position, she says, is that of loyal sons, not upstarts, and if they have been tactless he should forgive them like a loving father and "bear in mind that... being so far away, you do not understand things as well as I do here, and that although we women are not of much use as counsellors we are occasionally right". She herself, she adds, has received the General's directives through official channels in Madrid not in a personal communication. That has made the wound doubtly hurtful to her sensitivities:

> I will certainly not hide from your Reverence that, so far as I understand my own mind, it would have been a great satisfaction to me if you yourself had conveyed this order to me in a letter... I have been unable to help feeling hurt that I should have been treated like someone who has been very disobedient.[12]

Naturally, she says, she is more than willing to obey his command and retire to a convent. She will be grateful for a rest and intends to travel to Castile as soon as winter is past. Her great sorrow is that she cannot see him and explain the build up of misunderstanding in person: "So I shall have to wait for this happiness until that endless eternity in which your Reverence will discover how much you are to me. May the Lord in his mercy grant that I may merit it."[13]

On this sad note Teresa ended. She loved Rubeo, felt deep gratitude to him, and the breach, which was never healed (owing to his death) caused her grief to the end.

Preparations were made for the journey to Toledo. There, from her cell in the Carmel, the granddaughter of the Toledan Jew, Juan Sanchez, who ninety years before had walked the familiar streets as a purveyor of fine silks, sat in a patched serge habit and followed the fortunes of the Discalced. She kept in constant touch with Gratian and her prioresses by letter. Nothing was too much trouble for her; no concern too slight to merit her attention. And at Toledo she began her great masterpiece the *Interior Castle*. Her world might seem to be collapsing around her but the inner citadel held firm.

NOTES

1. Cf *Foundations*, ch. 24.
2. Ibid.
3. Ibid.
4. Ibid.
5. *Letter*, 93.
6. *Letter*, 94a.
7. *Letter*, 99.
8. *Letter*, 171.
9. *Letter*, 185.
10. *Letter*, 78.
11. Cf*Letter*, 204.
12. *Letter*, 91.
13. Ibid.

All glorious within

The Interior Castle. 1577

The pressures under which Teresa laboured at Toledo were
immense. Her whole life's work was at stake and, as
she was unable to be personally present to those who
needed her, the load of letter writing that fell to her lot
was well-nigh overwhelming. Several times she refers to
feeling unable to cope with all her correspondence. She
wishes it were burned or at the bottom of the sea "for I
have had so many letters during the last two days that they
have driven me crazy".[1] Seldom was she able to retire
before midnight. Her eminent position as foundress iso-
lated her, and in a moment of loneliness she wrote patheti-
cally to Gratian:

> I have been wondering which of the two your Paternity
> loves better – Señora Doña Juana (his mother) who, I
> reflected, has a husband and her other children to love
> her, or poor Laurencia (Teresa) who has no one else in
> the world but you, her father. May it please God to
> preserve him to her.[2]

Living in a regular convent Teresa was bound to a strict
timetable of Office in choir, personal prayer and manual
labour. Even in the parlour she would have her spinning at
hand so as to be able to contribute to the daily finances. No
wonder that by January 1577 she was ill with exhaustion
and following a prescribed course of "bleeding". With her
physical weakness went an increase in psychic phenomena
such as ecstasies, which further sapped her strength as she
struggled to resist these outward seisures. She felt ashamed
and embarrassed when they occurred in public.[3]

The book of her *Life* was still with the Inquisition and reports were reassuring on that score:

> The Grand Inquisitor himself is reading (my papers) which is something new. Somebody must have praised them to him; and he told Doña Luisa that there was nothing in them about which they would need to interfere: there was no harm in them – in fact, there was good.[4]

But the fact remained that this book, her most complete treatise to date on the later stages of prayer, was unavailable to her nuns. Gratian therefore persuaded her to tackle another treatise which would include the more advanced states to which she had attained since the *Life* was completed. The request of someone she loved as she loved Gratian mobilised Teresa to gather her strength and exert herself on the project, for love, human and divine, was the source of her creativity. Carmelite life was a life of prayer; it was for this that her nuns had come together in the Order. Whatever else might be happening prayer must ever have the primacy. So was begun *The Interior Castle*.

Teresa wrote her *opus magnum* in two stages. She began it as she says on the feast of the Holy Trinity, June 2nd 1577 after a vision of the beauty of the soul which is the dwelling of the Godhead (i.e. her own soul).[5] This was in Toledo. Towards the end of June the papal nuncio, Ormaneto, who was favourable to the Reform, died. Teresa then travelled to St Joseph's in Avila where her presence was henceforth required and where she spent the remainder of her years of enforced seclusion. The manuscript was not taken up again until the beginning of November:

> God help me in this task which I have embarked upon (she wrote at the beginning of the second chapter of the Fourth Mansion). I had quite forgotten what I was writing about, for business matters and ill health forced me to postpone continuing it until a more suitable time and,

128

as I have a poor memory, it will all be very confused, for
I cannot read it through again.

By the end of November the book was finished. In all
she had spent a bare six weeks in writing it; an almost
superhuman feat when one thinks of the confusion surrounding her, the lack of uninterrupted leisure and her
concern for the future of the Discalced. It was as if a child
was a-borning and the labour involved just *had* to proceed
come what may.

In her *Epilogue* Teresa says how glad she is to have
completed the work even though she began it with reluc-
tance. With tongue in cheek she assures her sisters that they
can explore their own "interior castle" whenever they wish.
No matter how strictly cloistered they are no superior can
prevent them having liberty there!

Meanwhile the nuns of the Incarnation had tried to
persuade Teresa to return to them for a second term as
prioress, thus incurring abuse and excommunication for
themselves from the new Vicar General, Tostado who,
together with the recently appointed nuncio, Sega, was
implacably opposed to the Reform. Five days after the
book's completion, John of the Cross was kidnapped and
removed to an unknown destination (actually Toledo) for
monastic imprisonment and perhaps, as Teresa feared, even
death. Yet here is *La Madre* writing at her best and assur-
ing her sisters that "once you have been shown how to
enjoy this castle you will find rest in everything, even in
things which most try you".[6]

The *Interior Castle* is a genuine blend of psychology
and theology, for Teresa writes as always from personal
experience. She writes too for her own sisters, taking prayer
as her subject and speaking as woman to woman, for
"women best understand each others language".[7] Her nuns
will understand because they are united to her by mutual
love and a common way of life. Teresa wants to share
herself with them and this she does primarily by recounting
the path she has taken to reach God and her observation of

others taking a similar route. She is not teaching methodical theology but sharing her own experience in conversational style, using myriad images to flesh out the basic pattern. In the *Interior Castle* are found her most celebrated metaphors: the palmito, the castle, the bee, the tortoise, the silkworm (already discussed elsewhere) and the waxen seal. Like the parables of the Gospel each can be meditated on individually, each one encapsulating as it does some aspect of Christian life. It is for the reader to make her own application. Not all will be led exactly alike for the Lord is sovereignly free; his largesse is not bounded by our finite minds and preconceived patterns.

In the book Teresa divides spiritual progress between seven "mansions" or sets of rooms which represent three stages of the life of prayer (which for Teresa is always 'life' in its widest sense). The first three mansions devolve on what *we* can do to move towards the central room where God dwells: carefulness in avoiding sin, growth in love for others, renunciation of the tendency to judge people, self-knowledge, humility, the activation of desire, the process of interiorisation. Mansion Four marks a transitional stage when God begins to take over and the soul responds to his touch. Mansions Five through Seven are where God purifies the soul fully that it may be configured to the likeness of Christ in the state of Spiritual Marriage.

As Teresa says, she writes of her *own* journey. There are other mansions which she has not described for God can never be exhausted by the experience of one person alone. John of the Cross puts it another way.

There are in Christ great depths to be fathomed, for he is a rich mine, with many recesses full of treasures, and however deeply we descend we shall never reach the end, for in every recess new veins of new treasures abound in every direction... The soul longs to enter in earnest into these caverns of Christ, that it may be transformed and inebriated in the love and knowledge of his mysteries, hiding itself in the bosom of the Beloved.[8]

Contact with Christ enriches rather than narrows life. In him is all fullness, joy and perfection and to find him we must enter within ourselves where he has his home. As we discover ourselves so we discover him and vice versa.

As I see it (writes Teresa) we shall never succeed in knowing ourselves unless we seek to know God. Let us think of his greatness and then come back to our own baseness... In speaking of the soul we must always think of it as spacious, ample and lofty; and this can be done without exaggeration for the soul's capacity is much greater than we can realise, and the Sun which is in the palace reaches every part of it.[9]

Meditation makes us present to self and to God, enlarging all our capacities, making us grow to full stature as persons. Teresa sees woman as both "castle" and "inwardness". It is the image preferred by a Christian feminist of our own century, Edith Stein, who said in a paper addressing the principles of women's education:

Woman succeeds... if the soul is empty of self and self-contained. Indeed, when the inherent, agitated self is completely gone, there is room and quiet to make oneself perceptible to others... "O Lord my God, take me away from myself and give me completely to you alone", the ancient German prayer says. We can do nothing of ourselves; God must do it. To speak to him thus is easier by nature for woman than for man because a natural desire lives in her to give herself completely to someone. When she has once realised that no-one other than God is capable of receiving her completely for himself... then the surrender is no longer difficult and she becomes free of herself. Then it is also self-evident to her to enclose herself in her castle, whereas before she was given to the storms which penetrated her from without again and again... Now she has all she needs; she reaches out when she is sent, and opens up only to that which may find admittance to her. She is mistress of this castle as the handmaid of the Lord and she is ready as handmaid for all whom the Lord desires her to serve. But above all this means she is ready to give herself to him who was given to her as visible sovereign – for her spouse or, also, for those having authority over her in some way or another.[10]

Other factors which Edith Stein recognises as especially applicable to women are enumerated in various ways in Teresa's writings. The soul of woman must be expansive, quiet, warm, clear, mistress of itself including its body, so that the entire person is at the disposal of every call. This total, all-inclusive spirituality is necessary for women who are more dependant on their bodies than are men and who must therefore adopt a way of following Christ which, while not negating the mind, includes heart, emotions and the power of loving.

All these elements can be found in Teresa's *Interior Castle*. They bring her therefore into a relationship of immediacy with women who seek a life of prayer even in the midst of professional responsibilities and the stresses of the modern world. Teresa never thought women were second class. She expected and demanded of them the best, felt they were worthy of being challenged to reach the heights.

As Teresa laboured at this period of her life with such intensity for her Discalced sons and daughters it is possible that she discerned in her body the first symptoms of the disease that was finally to kill her – cancer of the womb.

Her health had indeed been failing for some time. At Christmas, just a few weeks after finishing *The Interior Castle*, Teresa fell downstairs and dislocated her left arm. She had been feeling "old and tired", now she was helpless. Never again was she able to dress herself or take care of her personal needs. It was some time even before anyone could be found to set the arm, and the operation was carried out with such crudity that it caused her intolerable pain. Anne of St Bartholomew, a young lay sister, became her companion and nurse. She shared her cell, washed and dressed her, took care of her with a daughter's devotion. Through the remaining years Teresa and Anne were to become inseparable. There blossomed between them a tender intimacy all the more surprising for their different backgrounds and ages. Anne was a pure Spaniard of peasant stock, brought up close to the earth. Gratian teased her in that she had been more open with him about her forebears than Teresa (he did not know of Teresa's Jewish ancestry which she took good care to conceal from him). Anne was stalwart, proud, an indefatigable worker, illiterate until required to be her mentor's amanuensis. Teresa on her side was a woman of outstanding intellectual gifts, admired by the elite of the realm. Yet through their relationship many of Teresa's fine qualities were gradually imbibed by Anne who, after *La Madre*'s death would take Carmel to France, become a prioress herself, and eventually receive the honours of the church in her own beatification.

NOTES

1. *Letter*, 111.
2. Ibid.
3. Cf *Letter*, 163.
4. *Letter*, 171.
5. Cf *Interior Castle*, Mansion 1, ch. 1.
6. *Interior Castle*, Epilogue.
7. *Interior Castle*, Prologue.
8. *Spiritual Canticle*, Stanza 37 (Lewis translation).
9. *Interior Castle*, Mansion 1, ch. 2.
10. *Principles of Women's Education*. An article in *Woman*. Collected Works of Edith Stein no. 2, translated by Freda Mary Oben.

Two years of Upheaval

The battle for the Discalced cause. 1578-79

The new year dawned clear and cold, bringing with it no amelioration of trials. The nuns of the Incarnation were still agitating to have Teresa as prioress (though this eventually came to nothing) and her arm remained painful, swollen and encased in "a saffron plaster like a coat of mail".[1] Fortunately the frosts of Avila were not so bitter as in Toledo and Gratian, with tender concern, had arranged for an extra door to be added to the little room beside the imfirmary so the place was "as hot as an oven".[2] Teresa for her part worried over Gratian travelling in the bad weather and never lost the fear that he might be poisoned by his enemies. For a time he refused all food except eggs for this reason. It would seem that in religion anything goes as long as the cause is deemed to be the right one!

The papal nuncio Sega, who favoured the Calced, had initiated a policy of great severity. Soon all the leading friars of the Reform – Gratian, Antonio, Mariano and others were recipients of his wrath and spent various periods in hiding or in disgrace. As for John of the Cross, he was still held incommunicado, incarcerated in a tiny, airless cell, from which he was taken three times a week to receive a public scourging before the assembled community of the Toledo monastery.

Briefs were issued to halt the Reform. Other briefs were forthwith issued by the Royal Council annulling those of Sega. Negotiations dragged on. Teresa saw with ever greater clarity that the only solution would be the formation of a separate province for the Discalced. Her friars, frustrated and impatient at the delays, decided to go ahead without proper authorisation. They called a Chapter at Almodovar to declare a *fait accompli*. John of the Cross, recently escaped from imprisonment was also present, the marks of the discipline still raw on his emaciated body. He, like Teresa, protested that the Chapter was unauthorised and therefore without power, but his pleas went unheeded. She, having been appraised of John's ordeal felt this should at least arouse the nuncio's pity. She wrote to Gratian in indignation:

I can tell you I keep thinking of what they did to fray John of the Cross. I don't know how God can allow such things... For all these nine months he has been in a little cell, which would hardly hold him, small though he is; and all that time, though he had been at death's door, he never once changed his tunic. (Teresa seems more concerned at the lack of cleanliness than the corporal punishment!)... I envy him keenly. Our Lord indeed gave him abundant stores of strength for such a martyrdom... Information should be laid before the nuncio to show him what these people did with this saint of a fray John... It is a piteous story.[3]

But Sega, notwithstanding the evidence, continued to oppose the Reform.

The Discalced, certain that their only hope lay in recourse to Rome where they could personally present their case, voted to send two of their number (one of them Doria) to plead before the General. Before they set out news arrived that Rubeo was dead, the one man upon whom Teresa had pinned her hopes. "On the day I heard it I wept and wept – I could do nothing else – and I felt very much distressed at all the trouble we had caused him which he certainly did not deserve"[4] she confided to Gratian. Under such circumstances it seemed useless to send friars to Rome; they would only be arrested as fugitives and vagabonds, lose their documents and be the victims of their own inexperience.

Those who had participated in the Almodovar Chapter were summarily excommunicated and in December Sega announced that the Discalced were to be henceforth subject to the fathers of the mitigated observance.

It seemed as if all was lost, yet Teresa pushed on "I have not lost a jot of my confidence that everything will turn out well"[5] she declared. In a different context she reveals her indomitable spirit to the nuns of Seville:

> Courage, courage, my daughters. Remember, God gives no one more trouble than he is able to bear and he is with those who are in tribulation. That being so, you have no reason to fear: you must trust in his mercy that he will reveal the whole truth... Do not be distressed.[6]

Sure enough the storm began to subside. The King, always favourable to Teresa's cause, appointed a commission to examine the lives led by the Discalced (Philip was averse to the nuncio having the last word in his Majesty's domains). The commission included friends of Teresa's. She was jubilant at the news. Then on 1 April 1579 Fr Angel de Salazar was named Vicar General pending the erection of the Discalced into a separate province. Gratian was restored to his position and delegates chosen once more to travel to Rome. It was rumoured that the new Carmelite General was disposed to listen sympathetically to their cause.

Teresa remained throughout at St Joseph's. There were dificulties among the nuns at Seville, factions among the friars. She watched helplessly from the sidelines, praying, writing, scolding, exhorting by turns. But the tide was turning. In June of that year Fr Angel gave her permission to continue her visitation of convents and to found new ones. Teresa had mellowed and learned more about human nature. She set out, not to impose discipline but to spread love: this she was convinced was the only way to obtain a response worthy of a committed Christian.

> You know, I no longer govern in the way I used to. Love does everything. I am not sure if that is because no one

gives me cause to reprove her, or because I have discovered that things go better that way.[7]

Wherever Teresa went she was greeted with joy by her sisters, so long deprived of their foundress's presence and often subjected to the whims of inexperienced prioresses for "(Superiors) must not think they can first give an order and then countermand it, as married people do".[8] Advising, consoling, smoothing over difficulties, ever attended by her "dear Anne" Teresa observed all with the wisdom of age.

At Malagon, where the sisters were to move house after a troubled history under an unsuitable superior, *La Madre* threw herself into preparations even though she felt as if there were not a bone in her body that was not aching[9] after the journey. It was just like the old days when she was inseparable from bucket and mop. Her labour was well rewarded by the sight of a clean convent ready to welcome the Blessed Sacrament brought in solemn procession and all the sisters "...very happy: they looked just like lizards coming out into the sunshine in summer".[10] Her keen wit never flagged for it was in fact early December!

Teresa stayed at Malagon for Christmas. Two years before on Christmas Eve she had injured her arm. Last year at the same time she had cried bitterly over the disgrace of Gratian and the impending ruin of her Order; Anne reports that she wept through the whole Office of Matins. Now she is once more on the road, but memories still linger. How true it is that tragedies which transpire in a festive season bite doubly deep into the emotions.

Looking out from her cell window in Malagon's new convent she remembers it all. This will be a happy Christmas, she feels. Nevertheless she misses her dear "Paul". Her joy would be complete if only she could be with him at this time, able to hear his sermons which she is sure are excellent.[11] At Christmas everyone wants to be with their loved ones and Teresa was no exception. But God's work must come first.

NOTES

1. *Letter*, 111.
2. Ibid.
3. Cf *Letter*, 163.
4. *Letter*, 171.
5. Cf *Interior Castle*, Mansion 1, ch. 1.
6. *Interior Castle*, Epilogue.
7. *Interior Castle*, Prologue.
8. *Spiritual Canticle*, Stanza 37 (Lewis translation).
9. *Interior Castle*, Mansion 1, ch. 2.
10. *Principles of Women's Education*. An article in *Woman*. Collected Works of Edith Stein no. 2, translated by Freda Mary Oben.

Last years

The foundations of Villeneuva de la Jara, Palencia, Soria, Granada, Burgos. 1580-82

Having put her established convents in order Teresa channelled her energy towards further foundations: Villeneuva de la Jara where, as in Beas, she was welcomed rapturously by a group of *beatas*; Palencia, from whence Teresa heard the good news that her friars, holding their first official Chapter, had elected Gratian as Provincial; Soria, Burgos... while Anne of Jesus and John of the Cross founded a house in Granada. Teresa's appreciation of John had grown, of all the friars he was the only one who never caused her sorrow:

> Fray John of the Cross is considered by everybody, and by all the sisters, as a saint, and I do not think they are rating him too highly. In my opinion he is a tower of strength.[1]

It would be instructive could we know more of their intimate correspondence but John, in an effort to attain complete detachment of heart, burnt all her letters, and we have to be satisfied with the few references to him in her other epistles to friends and friars.

There was still plenty to trouble Teresa. Her brother Lorenzo died and disputes about his will erupted, causing a family feud in which she tried to act as mediator. Journeys took her through rain and snow, burning heat and biting cold, the inconvenience of inns and unremitting labour at her destination. Anne lifted her tenderly from the jolting carts in her strong arms, staunched the ever increasing haemmorhages, wrote letters by dictation. When there was a spare moment she washed Teresa's linen to

139

ensure cleanliness and freshness for her patient. Often, instead of sleeping, she would sit by *La Madre*'s bed, alert for her least wish, happy when she could provide some extra comfort or treat – a few tasty sweetmeats (Teresa had a very sweet tooth!) or fragrantly scented water to refresh her after her travels. Despite popular acclaim and the undoubted love of her ordinary sisters, Teresa was not always understood and accepted by her prioresses who could resent what they deemed an intrusion into the affairs of 'their' house. Her human loneliness and disappointment in these encounters was assuaged by her reliance on Anne and Gratian who provided the expressed affection she craved in her old age.

Her last foundation, Burgos, the chronicler described as Teresa's "crown of thorns and roses" as she faced the last months of her life. How far she had come since those days when she took her first steps in religious life as a novice at the Incarnation. Then all had been promise, a tiny seed buried in the soil of Mount Carmel. Now the plant was in bloom. Her houses were flourishing, her sisters numerous. But the blossom concealed the briars of suffering. Teresa was no longer vigorous and her presence, while honoured, was often greeted with a kindly smile and the deference due to the elderly, rather than with the respect accorded her in the days of her strength. "I have a little more experience than you" she wrote to her beloved Maria de San José "but little more notice will be taken of me now. You would be shocked to see how old I am and how little use for anything".[2] She was disappointed too that her attempts to found in Madrid, the nation's capital, had come to nought. That would be accomplished by others after her death.

Teresa travelled to Burgos with Gratian and she describes the foundation of the Carmel there with all her accustomed asperity. There is no hint that her end was approaching. It is a lively tale, full of conflict and drama, lightened by the presence of her "Paul" whose placid temperament she never ceases to laud and which counteracts the overexcitability of the nuns who are nearly drowned trying to cross a swollen river.[3]

Journeying in terrible weather, her throat hardly better than an open wound, her tongue inflamed and paralysed, Teresa and her companions arrived in the city where "the storms had been so heavy the streets were like rivers".[4] They went first to pray before the famous crucifix in the Church of the Augustinian fathers – the Christ of Burgos. It was an image such as Teresa loved, wondrous in its pathos and realism, reputed to have been carved by the biblical Nicodemus. Here before Christ on the Cross Teresa knelt to commend her venture to the Saviour. Her imagination stirred at the sight of the embroidered curtains being drawn back to reveal the figure of the Crucified, his dark, thorncrowned head illumined by the glimmer of a hundred lamps and sixty silver candlesticks.

Wet and cold the group presently alighted at the home of their benefactress, the widow Catalina de Tolosa. She had kindled a fire to welcome them and dry their clothes after the trip. The thought was kindly but the smoke affected Teresa adversely. Next day, following a night of giddiness and vomiting blood, she could scarcely raise her head. Nevertheless, civil and ecclesiastical dignitaries had come to greet her and out of courtesy she needs must speak with them. This she did lying on her bed before a barred and curtained window. No matter how she felt, business had to be transacted as usual; and in this case there was an advantage to being an enclosed nun – her hiddenness did not even arouse comment!

The Archbishop, upon whose good will Teresa had counted, manifested displeasure at her presence and refused consent for the proposed convent, notwithstanding her long journey and the fact that she had brought other nuns with her. He said they might as well return the way they glad come. "The roads of course were charming and it was such nice weather!"[5] she observed ironically, quailing at the thought yet finding room for a laugh and an 'aside' to the Lord:

O my Lord, how true it is that as soon as a person renders you some service he is rewarded with great trials! And what a priceless reward they are for those of us who truly love you, if only we recognised their value at the time![6]

She was well practised in finding trials valuable. Meanwhile negotiations stalled and the Archbishop remained unmoved. In his judgment "his city stood in no need of reformation, the monasteries and convents in it being quite reformed enough already".[7]

The nuns, forbidden to hear Mass in Catalina's house, had to go daily through the streets, muddy and dirty as they were, to a neighbouring church. It was inconvenient for all, and Gratian, whose presence had been relied on, found himself compelled to leave for an engagement of Lenten sermons in Valladolid. Before he departed however, he was able to arrange the nuns' lodgings in the Hospital of the Conception, a great rambling building in a sandy suburb. Here, installed in an attic, troubled by vermin and the odour of departed patients whose nursing care had been none too fastidious, Teresa settled down joyfully exclaiming "Do not pity me, for the Lord suffered more when he drank the gall and vinegar",[8] a reference to the bloody wound in her throat which made eating painful and difficult. One day, sick and discouraged, she longed for an orange to refresh her; but on receiving it she merely descended to the hospital where she divided the fruit among some inmates as a treat.

When she was well enough to go about Teresa busied herself scouring Burgos for a suitable residence while her benefactress stood surety for an endowment. Teresa was determined to succeed. She had come to Burgos to found a convent of Discalced nuns and her resolution could be not deflected.

Finally things began to fall into place. A building was found and purchased, the Archbishop mollified, the first Mass celebrated. It was 19th April 1582. Teresa was sixty-seven. From behind her enveloping black veil her face, wrinkled and worn, shone with happiness. The minstrels and musicians of Burgos swelled the parade (Teresa could never resist a good spectacle). The nuns, thankful at last to find themselves in a proper enclosure sighed with relief. The foundress wrote:

> Only those who have experienced it will believe what pleasure we get...when we find ourselves at last in a cloister which can be entered by no one from the world. For, however much we may love those in the world, our love is not enough to deprive us of our great happiness when we find ourselves alone. It is as when a great many fish are taken from the river in a net: they cannot live unless they are put back in the river. Even so it is with souls accustomed to live in the streams of the water of their Spouse... O Very Man and Very God, my Spouse! Is this a favour to be regarded lightly? Let us praise him my sisters for having granted it to us... May he be blessed forever. Amen. Amen.[9]

These words come from the pen of a woman who for most of her later life dealt with business matters as if she were a modern executive. Yet her heart was as solitary in its depths as those of the first hermits of Mount Carmel she so revered and whose habit she humbly declared herself unworthy to wear.

Teresa remained at Burgos until the end of July. She had dedicated her convent under the patronage of St Joseph her old friend, and St Anne the Lord's grandmother. It seems that as she aged her devotion to this latter saint grew apace and she departed from the city on her feast day.

The sisters gathered to wish her God-speed. Teresa was to travel with Anne and her now teenage niece Teresita, due to make her vows in Avila when they arrived back. The delightful child had grown into a somewhat morose young woman, her problems aggravated by the death of her father Lorenzo and resultant disputes about her dowry.

Leavetaking was a replay of similar occasions, made even more touching by the obvious fact that Teresa was old and infirm. These emotional scenes were a trial for her, a tug at the heart as she witnessed the tears of those left behind:

I love them so much that I assure you that was not the least of my crosses, particularly when I thought I might never see them again and how sorry they were and how they wept. For, though they are detached from all else, God has not granted them detachment in this, perhaps in order that it may be a greater torment to me. Nor am I detached from them, though I have always done my utmost not to show this, and indeed rebuked them for their attachment. But this did little good for their love for me is very deep and there are many ways in which it can be seen how true it is.[10]

The old woman brushed aside her own tears and entered the waiting conveyance, her helpless arm supported by the everfaithful Anne. Black veil and white veil side by side they set off. It was to be Teresa's final journey. She opened her breviary to read the psalms appointed for the day. She found them indicated by a marker bearing the legend:

Let nothing disturb you,
Nothing affright you,
All things pass away.
God alone abideth.
Patience obtains all things.
Whoever has God can want for nothing,
God alone sufficeth.

The covered cart rolled through the city gates and out onto the plain beyond. Avila was her destination, but she did not know she would not live to see it again.

NOTES

1. *Letter*, 210.
2. *Letter*, 410.
3. Cf *Foundations*, ch. 31.
4. Testimony of Anne of St Bartholomew in *Appendix* to the *Complete Works*.
5. *Foundations, ch.* 31.
6. Ibid.
7. Testimony of Anne of St Bartholomew, *op. cit.*
8. Ibid.
9. *Foundations*, ch. 31.
10. *Foundations*, ch. 27.

Ad paradisum

Final journey and death at Alba de Tormes.
July-October 1582

It was an itinerary filled with bitter disappointments. Teresa had counted on Gratian's companionship but he pleaded commitments in Andalusia. Unable to hide the hurt she felt she wrote poignantly:

> The reasons you gave for your decision to go there did not seem to me sufficient... So keenly did I feel your being away at such a time that I lost the desire to write to you... I had a perfectly wretched night and my head is bad this morning... Oh, how sorry (Teresita) was your Reverence did not come... She will begin to understand how little trust one can place in anyone but God... With God's help we shall be in Avila by the end of the month. Believe me, it would never do to drag that girl about from one place to another any longer. Oh my father, how oppressed I have been feeling lately! But the oppression passed off when I heard that you were well. May God be pleased to prosper you henceforward.[1]

The route was to include stops at Palencia, Valladolid and Medina where various problems needed Teresa's intervention. She was also troubled by news of Anne of Jesus mishandling the Granada foundation. Just when she wanted rest and peace she had to turn her attention to squabbles and lawsuits. At Valladolid her niece Maria Bautista, companion and friend from the earliest days at St Joseph's, sided with Teresa's enemies in contesting Lorenzo's will. Deeply wounded at Maria's coldness and harsh manner the foundress prepared to depart. As she passed out of the enclosure the prioress caught hold of Anne's habit and

146

appraised her of the fact that they would not be welcomed again should they dare return to the place.

At Medina likewise the insubordination of the prioress cut Teresa's sensitive heart which so loved to have its love requited. She had helped her daughters in all their trials, now they were acting like adolescents wanting to be free of every constraint. Had her prayer-life been less genuine it would have evaporated beneath the strain. Among the friars Gratian and Doria were on the verge of a confrontation that would tear the Reform apart after Teresa's death. It was a final way of the cross. Many times she had exhorted her daughters to bear suffering bravely. Could she do less herself?

At last she turned thankfully towards Avila and St Joseph's. Soon she would be "home". But a further disappointment met her even as she envisaged the familiar cell and cloisters in her native city. A message arrived from Antonio of Jesus, the Provincial: the duchess of Alba had sent her coach to convey *la Santa* to her palace. She wished her to be present to bless the confinement of her daughter-in-law and pray for a safe delivery.

Teresa felt too broken to resist. Nor could she disobey the heartless order of her Provincial superior, that same Antonio who, despite her fears that he was not able for an austere life, lived to be over ninety!

Anne and her charge set out for Alba. It was a slow trek across the Castilian plain that autumn. The landscape, bare but for grapes and white hawthorn fruit, presaged the long winter and the promise of another spring. Teresa was dying. Anne was distraught. She tried to procure some soft food for the invalid but could only get some dried figs, hard and withered. Anne desperately offered all she had for eggs, none could be purchased anywhere. "Do not be afflicted daughter" murmured the intrepid old lady, seeing tears of pity coursing down her companion's face and staining her linen toque, "These figs are good and there are many poor people who do not get such a treat". Another day the only food was boiled onions with greenstuff.[2] Anne longed for the journey to end and for Teresa to be safely in bed – never mind the duchess!

At last the grey city of Alba hove in sight above the swelling river Tormes. Teresa was like Pilgrim looking towards the heavenly Jerusalem, ready to cross over where the trumpets would sound a welcome. But the only welcome was a message from the duchess – my lady had already been safely delivered. "Thank God then that this saint will no longer be needed" quipped Teresa with a spark of her old spirit.

Gratefully she drove to the convent where a loving community awaited her. Contrary to custom she allowed the sisters to kiss her hand and offer other marks of endearment. She was undressed and put to bed. "Oh God help me" she exclaimed, "How tired I feel. It is more than twenty years since I went to bed so early. Blessed be God that I have fallen ill among you".

For the next eight days Teresa tried to resume her accustomed life: interviewing, inspecting, joining the sisters for prayer and recreation – but it could not last. On St Michael's day she sickened. Her failing strength could no longer be conquered by her will.

Patiently she submitted to the prescribed remedies, though she knew in herself they were of no avail. She would have been content just to have Anne's presence, to be nursed by her familiar hands, to have her linens changed by one so careful for her comfort and happiness.

Father Antonio arrived to hear her confession. The duchess of Alba insisted on helping with the nursing, remarking on the sweet smell emanating from her distinguished patient.

The end was approaching. At five o'clock on St Francis's Eve, 3rd October 1582 Teresa received the last Sacraments. She was surrounded by her Alba sisters, each holding a lighted candle:

Daughters and my mistresses (she whispered) I beseech you to pardon the bad example I have set you, who have been the greatest sinner in the world, and she who has kept her Rule and Constitutions the worst. I beseech you for the love of God my daughters to keep them with great perfection and obey your superiors.[3]

The Host was brought. Even at this stage the dying woman tried to raise herself to greet the Divine Lover. Clasping her hands she cried out: "Oh my Lord and Spouse, at last the longed for hour has come; at last we shall see each other!" Gradually she entered into a trance, protesting over and over "I am a daughter of the Church", and murmuring the words of the psalmist, "A humbled contrite heart O God you will not spurn".

If it is true that before death scene's from one's life pass before the inner eye, how many scenes must have passed before hers. The guileless child playing with her brother and longing for martyrdom; the beautiful and flirtatious girl, toast of society; the young nun radiant on her Profession day; her illness unto death; her conversion before the Christ at the pillar; the days at St Joseph's; the journeyings, the friendships, the joys and disappointments of a full life...

She was recalled from her reverie by the pompous Antonio asking where she wished to be buried. "Jesus" she exclaimed weakly – adding with a sigh "Can you not spare me here a little earth?"

Then she lapsed into unconsciousness. The nuns kept vigil by turns. The candles burned continuously. The bare cell was the focal point of the whole house. All else seemed to come to a standstill. It was the feast of St Francis, that outstanding lover of the crucified Saviour. Teresa had always revered him and St Clare for their poverty and single-minded dedication. Now she lay in her turn, a poor woman, dependent on those surrounding her, silent and unmoving.

Anne remained at her side: sleepless, attentive, weary from constant nursing.

Antonio signed to her to get something to eat, but no sooner had Anne slipped from the room than Teresa anxiously turned her head on the pillow. Anne hastened back.

A smile passed over the lips of the dying nun. She clasped the two hands of her devoted infirmarian. She raised her head, placing it in Anne's arms. Anne held her thus cradled until the breathing ceased. It was towards nine on the night of 4 October 1582.

Teresa de Ahumada, granddaughter of the Jew Juan Sanchez, contemplative nun, restorer of the Primitive Rule of St Albert, foundress of the Discalced Carmelites, died as plain Teresa of Jesus, *La Madre*.

...And the trumpets sounded for her on the other side.

NOTES

1. *Letter*, 434.
2. Details from Testimony of Anne of St Bartholomew, *op. cit.*
3. Testimony of Mother Maria de San Francisco. Quoted in *Santa Teresa*, p. 729.

Epilogue

1597

Fifteen years later, the Chapter of the Discalced Carmelites meeting in Madrid passed the following legislation for Spain, Portugal and Mexico.

Let the novices when they enter the Order give information about the purity of their ancestry so that in the investigation, following the questions of the *Motu Proprio* of Sixtus V, a specific question be put as to whether the candidate is of Jewish or Moorish descent at all or if he have any ancestors up to the fourth generation inclusive who were *confessos* or *penitenciados*. When the novice has given this information, let him be advised in secret before taking the habit that should anything contrary to this testimony be discovered, the Order is free to expel him, and that his Profession will be null and void, because the Order does not accept it. And let him be advised of the same in the final examination prior to Profession.

* * * * *

The soul sometimes enjoys a quiet laugh when it sees serious people... making a great fuss about niceties concerning their honour... It realises that genuine honour is not deceptive but true; that it values what has worth and despises what has none; for what passes away and is not pleasing to God is worth nothing and less than nothing.

St Teresa

Appendix

THE "PRIMITIVE" RULE OF THE ORDER OF THE
BLESSED VIRGIN MARY OF MOUNT CARMEL
GIVEN BY ST ALBERT,
PATRIARCH OF JERUSALEM
AND CORRECTED, EMENDED AND CONFIRMED
BY POPE INNOCENT IV

Albert, called by God's favour to be Patriarch of the Church
of Jerusalem, bids health in the Lord and the blessing of the
Holy Spirit to his beloved sons in Christ, B. and the other
hermits under obedience to him who live near the spring
(of Elias) on Mount Carmel.

Many and varied are the ways (cf. Hebr 1:1) in which
our saintly forefathers laid down how everyone, whatever
his station or the kind of religious observance he has chosen, should live a life of allegiance to Jesus Christ (cf. 2
Cor 10:5) – how pure in heart and steadfast in conscience
(cf. 1 Tim 1:5), he must be unswerving in the service of his
Master.

It is to me, however, that you have come for a rule of
life in keeping with your avowed purpose, a rule you may
hold fast to henceforward; and therefore:

(The Prior and profession)
The first thing I require is for you to have a Prior, one of
yourselves, who is to be chosen for the office by common
consent, or that of the greater and maturer part of you. Each
of the others must promise him obedience – of which, once
promised, he must try to make his deeds the true reflection
(cf. 1 John 3:18) – and also chastity and the renunciation of
ownership.

(Foundations)

If the Prior and brothers see fit, you have may foundations in solitary places, or where you are given a site that is
suitable and convenient for the observance proper to your
Order.

(The separate cells)

Next, each one of you is to have a separate cell, situated
as the lie of the land you propose to occupy may dictate,
and allotted by disposition of the Prior with the agreement
of the other brothers, or the more mature among them.

(The common refectory)

However, you are to eat whatever may have been given
you in a common refectory, listening together meanwhile
to a reading from Holy Scripture where that can be done
without difficulty.

(The Prior's authority)

None of the brothers is to occupy a cell other than that
allotted to him, or to exchange cells with another, without
leave of whoever is Prior at the time.

The Prior's cell should stand near the entrace to your
property, so that he may be the first to meet those who
approach, and whatever has to be done in consequence
may all be carried out as he may decide or order.

(Continual prayer)

Each of you is to stay in his own cell or nearby, pondering the Lord's law day and night (cf. Ps 1:2; Jos 1:8) and
keeping watch at his prayers (cf. 1 Pet 4:7) unless attending
to some other duty.

(The Canonical Hours)

Those who know how to say the canonical hours with
those in orders should do so, in the way those holy forefathers of ours laid down, and according to the Church's
approved custom.

Those who do not know the hours must say twenty-five "Our Fathers" for the night office, except on Sundays and solemnities when that number is to be doubled so that the "Our Father" is said fifty times; the same prayer must be said seven times in the morning in place of Lauds, and seven times too for each of the other hours, except for Vespers when it must be said fifteen times.

(Poverty and common life)

None of the brothers must lay claim to anything as his own but you are to possess everything in common (cf. Acts 4:32; 2:44); and each one is to receive from the Prior – that is from the brother he appoints for the purpose – whatever befits his age and needs (cf. Acts 4:35).

(Common possessions)

You may have as many asses and mules as you need, however, and may keep a certain amount of livestock or poultry.

(The oratory and daily mass)

An oratory should be built as conveniently as possible among the cells, where, if it can be done without difficulty, you are to gather each morning to hear Mass.

(Fraternal discussion and correction)

On Sundays too, or other days if necessary, you should discuss matters of discipline and your spiritual welfare; and on this occasion the indiscretions and failings of the brothers, if any be found at fault, should be lovingly corrected.

(Fasting)

You are to fast every day, except Sunday, from the feast of the Exaltation of the Holy Cross until Easter Day, unless bodily sickness or feebleness, or some other good reason, demand a dispensation from the fast; for necessity overrides every law.

(Abstinence)

You are to abstain from meat, except as a remedy for sickness or feebleness. But as, when you are on a journey, you more often than not have to beg your way, outside your own houses you may eat foodstuffs that have been cooked with meat, so as to avoid giving trouble to your hosts. At sea, however, meat may be eaten.

(Exhortations)

Since man's life on earth is a time of trial (cf. Job 7:1) and all who would live devotedly in Christ must undergo persecution (cf. 2 Tim 3:12), and the devil your foe is on the prowl like a roaring lion looking for prey to devour (cf. 1 Pet 5:8), you must use every care to clothe yourselves in God's armour so that you may be ready to withstand the enemy's ambush (cf. Eph 6:11).

Your loins are to be girt (cf. Eph 6:14) with chastity, your breast fortified by holy meditations, for, as Scripture has it: "Holy meditation will save you" (Prov 2:11). Put on holiness as your breastplate (cf. Eph 6:14), and it will enable you to love the Lord your God with all your heart and soul and strength (cf. Deut 6:5), and your neighbour as yourself (cf. Mt 19:19; 22:37-39).

Faith must be your shield on all occasions, and with it you will be able to quench all the flaming missiles of the wicked one (cf. Eph 6,16): there can be no pleasing God without faith (cf. Hebr 11:6). On your head set the helmet of salvation (cf. Eph 6:17), and so be sure of deliverance by our only Saviour, who sets his own free from their sins (cf. Mt 1:21).

The sword of the spirit, the word of God (cf. Eph 6:17), must abound (cf. Col 3:16) in your mouths and hearts (cf. Rom 10:8). Let all you do have the Lord's word for accompaniment (cf. Col 3:17; 1 Cor 10:31).

(Work)

You must give yourselves to work of some kind, so that the devil may always find you busy; no idleness on your part must give him a chance to pierce the defences of your souls. In this respect you have both the teaching and the example of St Paul the Apostle, into whose mouth Christ put his own words (cf. 2 Cor 13:3). God made him preacher and teacher of faith and truth to the nations (cf. 1 Tim 2:7): with him as your leader you cannot go astray.

"We lived among you – he said – labouring and weary, toiling night and day so as not to be a burden to any of you; not because we had no power to do otherwise but so as to give you, in our own selves, an example you might imitate. For the charge we gave you when we were with you was this: that whoever is not willing to work should not be allowed to eat either. for we have heard that there are certain restless idlers among you. We charge people of this kind, and implore them in the name of our Lord Jesus Christ, that they earn their own bread by silent toil" (2 Thess 3:7-12). This is the way of holiness and goodness: see that you follow it (cf. Is 30:21).

(Silence)

The Apostle would have us keep silence, for in silence he tells us to work (cf. 2 Thess 3:12). As the Prophet also makes known to us: "Silence is the way to foster holiness" (cf. Is 32:17). Elsewhere he says: "Your strength will lie in silence and hope" (cf. Is 20:15).

For this reason I lay down that you are to keep silence from after Compline until after Prime the next day. At other times, although you need not keep silence so strictly, be careful not to indulge in a great deal of talk, for, as Scripture has it – and experience teaches us no less – "Sin will not be wanting where there is much talk" (Prov 10:19), and "He who is careless in speech will come to harm" (Prov 13,3); and elsewhere; The use of many words brings harm to the speaker's soul (cf. Sir 20:8). And our Lord says in the Gospel: "Every rash word uttered will have to be accounted for on judgement day" (Mt 12:36).

Make a balance then, each of you, to weigh your words in; keep a tight rein on your mouths, lest you should stumble and fall in speech, and your fall be irreparable and prove mortal (cf. Sir 28:29-30). Like the Prophet, watch your step lest your tongue give offence (ct. Ps 38:2), and employ every care in keeping silent, which is the way to foster holiness (cf. Is 32:17).

(The Prior to be at the service of his brothers)

You, brother B., and whoever may succeed you as Prior, must always keep in mind and put into practice what our Lord said in the Gospel: "Whoever has a mind to become a leader among you must make himself servant to the rest, and whichever of you would be first must become your bondsman" (Mt 20:26-27; cf. Mk 10,43-44).

(The Prior to be honoured as Christ's representative)

You other brothers too, hold your Prior in humble reverence, your minds not on him but on Christ who has placed him over you, and who, to those who rule the Churches, addressed these words: "Whoever pays you heed pays heed to me, and whoever treats you with dishonour dishonours me" (Lk 10:16); if you remain so minded you will not be found guilty of contempt, but will merit life eternal as fit reward for your obedience.

(Epilogue)

Here are the few points I have written down to provide you with a standard of conduct to live up to; but our Lord, at his second coming, will reward anyone who does more than he is obliged to do. See that the bounds of common sense are not exceeded, however, for common sense is the guide of the virtues.

Bibliography

Allison Peers E., *The Complete Works of St Teresa of Jesus*, in 3 volumes, Sheed and Ward 1946.

Allison Peers E., *The Letters of St Teresa of Jesus*, in 2 volumes, Sheed and Ward 1980.

Allison Peers E., *Mother of Carmel*, S.C.M. Press Ltd 1945.

Alvarez T. and Domingo F., *St Teresa of Avila – A Spiritual Adventure*, ICS Publications USA 1981.

Carmelite Studies, *Symposium* (John Sullivan ed.), vol. 1: Spiritual Direction and Historical Studies, ICS Publications 1980.

Carmelite Studies, *Centenary of St Teresa,* ICS Publications 1984.

Clissold S.,*St Teresa of Avila*, Sheldon Press 1979.

Cunningham Graham G., *Santa Teresa Her Life and Times*, Eveleigh Nash 1907.

Duque B.J., *Anne of St Bartholomew*, Spain 1979.

Hamilton E., *The Great Teresa*, Chatto and Windus Ltd 1960.

Hardy R.P., *Search for Nothing – The Life of St John of the Cross*, DLT 1987.

Stein E., *Collected Works*, vol. 2: translated by Freda Mary Oben, ICS Publications 1987.

Teresa's own writings

The Book of her Life
The Way of Perfection
Conceptions of the Love of God
The Interior Castle
Relations
Exclamations
The Book of Foundations
Guidelines for the Visitation of Convents
Primitive Constitutions
Letters